Spotlight on Young Children

Social & Emotional Development

Revised Edition

Marilou Hyson EDITOR

National Association for the Education of Young Children
Washington, DC

National Association for the Education of Young Children

1401 H Street NW, Suite 600
Washington, DC 20005
202-232-8777 • 800-424-2460
NAEYC.org

NAEYC Books

**Senior Director, Publishing
& Content Development**
Susan Friedman

Director, Books
Dana Battaglia

Senior Editor
Holly Bohart

Editor II
Rossella Procopio

Senior Creative Design Manager
Charity Coleman

Senior Creative Design Specialist
Gillian Frank

Creative Design Specialist
Makayla Johnson

Creative Design Specialist
Ashley McGowan

**Publishing Business
Operations Manager**
Francine Markowitz

Through its publications program, the National Association for the Education of Young Children (NAEYC) provides a forum for discussion of major issues and ideas in the early childhood field, with the hope of provoking thought and promoting professional growth. The views expressed or implied in this book are not necessarily those of the Association.

Permissions

NAEYC accepts requests for limited use of our copyrighted material. For permission to reprint, adapt, translate, or otherwise reuse and repurpose content from this publication, review our guidelines at **NAEYC.org/resources/permissions.**

The following selections were previously published in the specified issues of *Teaching Young Children*: S. Warsi, "Welcoming Refugee Children into Early Childhood Classrooms," August/September 2017; A. Hooper, "Partnering with Families: Supporting Social and Emotional Development Through Picture Books," October/November 2020; and B.L. DelVecchio, S. Ferguson, and W. Knapp, "Using Nature Contact to Support Children Under Stress," Fall 2021.

The following selections were previously published in the specified issues of *Young Children*: A.S. Kennedy, "Supporting Peer Relationships and Social Competence in Inclusive Preschool Programs," November 2013; J.M. Raisor and S.D. Thompson, "Guidance Strategies to Prevent and Address Preschool Bullying," May 2014; K. Statman-Weil, "Creating Trauma-Sensitive Classrooms," May 2015; V.S. Collet, "'I Can Do That!' Fostering Resilience in Young Children," March 2017; L.M. Platas, "Three for One: Supporting Social, Emotional, and Mathematical Development in Preschool and Kindergarten," March 2017; J. Ho and S. Funk, "Promoting Young Children's Social and Emotional Health," March 2018; I. Alanís and M. Guadalupe Arreguín, "Paired Learning: Strategies for Enhancing Social Competence in Dual Language Classrooms," May 2019; S.L. Brown, A. Aberson, S. Easley, and K.E. McGoey, "Supporting Anxious Children in the Preschool Classroom," July 2020; V. Benavides, R. Ledda, and M. Mohammed, "Never Too Young to Champion a Cause: Supporting Positive Identity Development Through Social Justice Curriculum in Preschool," December 2020; and B.L. Wright, "What About the Children? Teachers Cultivating and Nurturing the Voice and Agency of Young Children," Summer 2021.

Cover Photo Credits

Library of Congress Control Number: 2022939993

ISBN: 978-1-952331-14-5

Item: 1164

Contents

Introduction

Marilou Hyson

Tonya, a first-year prekindergarten teacher in a child care center, greets the children and their families as they enter her room. She was hired at the last minute in the midst of staff shortages, and this is the first time she is meeting the children she will be teaching. Except for what she was able to learn from some class records, Tonya knows little about these children or their families. At her orientation, the administrators emphasized that many of the children are "far behind" in relation to the center's standards. Observing the children, she sees that some children are eager to make friends with new classmates, although perhaps unsure how. Two children appear to be teasing another child; Tonya watches closely to see how she might get involved. Some children seem hesitant to interact with Tonya when she greets them. A few children excitedly explore the books and puzzles provided for their use, but others seem reluctant to try. As she watches, Tonya, asks herself what her priorities should be. How should she think about learning goals? How can she support these children, each with their own interests, concerns, and characteristics? Who and what can she depend on for help as she begins this challenging new experience?

Children's social and emotional development has long been a central focus in child development and early childhood history, research, and policy advocacy (Lascarides & Hinitz 2011; Weissberg et al. 2015). Within that tradition, NAEYC has repeatedly emphasized this domain in its position statements and publications. Continuing this work, the fourth edition of *Developmentally Appropriate Practice* (NAEYC 2022) weaves support of social and emotional learning into the fabric of effective teaching, considering these priorities through cultural and contextual frameworks and a lens of equity.

A wide range of factors—including children's relationships, self-identity, sense of belonging, understanding of others, engagement in learning, and emotional well-being—form the foundation of children's later social and emotional development as well as their competence in other areas. The guidelines for developmentally appropriate practice (i.e., caring and equitable communities of learners, reciprocal family partnerships, assessment of development and learning, teaching practices, curriculum decisions, and professionalism) are intended to help educators support children's social and emotional growth as well as their development in other, interrelated domains.

Along with the publication of the fourth edition of *Developmentally Appropriate Practice,* new social and emotional knowledge, concerns, and issues have prompted this revised edition of *Spotlight on Young Children: Social and Emotional Development.*

Brain science and social and emotional development. *From Neurons to Neighborhoods* (NRC & IOM 2000) heightened attention to brain research as a window into early development. Recent advances in brain science have shown how children's social and emotional experiences in their families, schools, and communities may directly and indirectly impact the brain networks that are the basis of thinking and academic learning (e.g., Immordino-Yang, Darling-Hammond, & Krone 2018).

Cultural contexts of social and emotional development. As seen in the fourth edition of *Developmentally Appropriate Practice,* much wider and deeper recognition is being given to children's cultural contexts as central components of their social and emotional development. Now more than ever before, teachers are engaging in conversations, both in person and online, about the challenges and rewards of implementing culturally responsive approaches to social and emotional learning in the classroom (Ferlazzo 2021). Researchers, too, are highlighting the need for fair and equitable attention to the study of culture and its impacts on children. The journal *Early Education and Development* devoted an entire issue to the topic of cultural contexts of social and emotional development (Chung, Lam, & Liew 2022). In their introduction, the editors ask a pointed question: "If culture is all around us, where is it reflected in our theories and our research?"

Violence and young children's mental health. The effect of family, school, and community violence is another issue with a long history, with much recent attention being given to the severity of the impacts on young children and their mental health. In response, the *Social Policy Report* (Malti 2020) emphasizes how social and emotional protective factors may buffer the impact of violence and nurture mental health in every child. Early childhood programs can play a key role in providing this kind of social and emotional support.

Educators' social and emotional well-being. Concerns about teacher stress have been raised for years, but COVID-19 highlighted these issues with new urgency. *Early Education and Development* featured a collection of studies and commentaries specifically about early childhood professionals' social and emotional well-being (Jennings, Jeon, & Roberts 2020). In order for educators to nurture children's social and emotional development, educators' own feelings and relationships also need validation and support.

This volume brings together articles from the previous edition and additional articles that further address timely topics for the field. The articles are grouped into four parts, each focusing on an important priority for early childhood educators as they support the social and emotional development of children from birth through age 8:

> Part One: Identifying and Building Strengths

> Part Two: Building Caring, Peaceful Communities

> Part Three: Supporting Children and Families in Difficult Times

> Part Four: Integrating Social and Emotional Perspectives into the Curriculum

Each article is accompanied by questions prompting reflection and application. As you read these articles and consider their relevance in your work, you will sense the authors' passion for children's well-being and their solidly grounded, innovative suggestions for building strong social and emotional foundations. Draw upon their ideas and connect them with your own community contexts to create loving, equitable, and developmentally appropriate environments for each and every child.

REFERENCES

Chung, K.K.H., C.B. Lam, & J. Liew, eds. 2022. "Studying Children's Social-Emotional Development in School and at Home Through a Cultural Lens." *Early Education and Development* 33 (5).

Ferlazzo, L. 2021. "Culturally Responsive Social-Emotional Learning: How to Get There." *Education Week,* November 26. www.edweek.org/leadership/opinion-culturally-responsive-social-emotional-learning-how-to-get-there/2021/11.

Immordino-Yang, M.H., L. Darling-Hammond, & C. Krone. 2018. "The Brain Basis for Integrated Social, Emotional, and Academic Development: How Emotions and Social Relationships Drive Learning." Research brief. Washington, DC: The Aspen Institute. www.aspeninstitute.org/publications/the-brain-basis-for-integrated-social-emotional-and-academic-development.

Jennings, P.A., L. Jeon, & A.M. Roberts, eds. 2020. "Introduction to the Special Issue on Early Care and Education Professionals' Social and Emotional Well-Being." *Early Education and Development* 31 (7): 933–39.

Lascarides, V.C., & B.F. Hinitz. 2011. *History of Early Childhood Education.* New York: Routledge.

Malti, T. 2020. "Children and Violence: Nurturing Social-Emotional Development to Promote Mental Health." *Social Policy Report* 33 (2): 1–27.

NAEYC. 2022. *Developmentally Appropriate Practice in Early Childhood Programs Serving Children from Birth Through Age 8.* 4th ed. Washington, DC: NAEYC.

NRC (National Research Council) & IOM (Institute of Medicine). 2000. *From Neurons to Neighborhoods: The Science of Early Childhood Development.* Report. Washington, DC: National Academies Press.

Weissberg, R.P., J.A. Durlak, C.E. Domitrovich, & T.P. Gullotta. 2015. "Social and Emotional Learning: Past, Present, and Future." In *Handbook of Social and Emotional Learning: Research and Practice,* eds. J.A. Durlak, C.E. Domitrovich, R.P. Weissberg, & T.P. Gullotta, 3–19. New York: Guilford Press.

About the Editor

Marilou Hyson, PhD, consults nationally and internationally on early childhood issues, with special emphasis on emotional development and professional development for teachers. Formerly, Marilou was NAEYC's associate executive director for professional development, where she led the development of several position statements and standards. She has been a preschool and kindergarten teacher and a university teacher educator.

Identifying and
Building Strengths

A renewed emphasis on strengths-based approaches to early childhood research and practice requires educators to think more deeply about the social and cultural contexts of development and learning (NAEYC 2022). From this perspective, teachers' starting point in nurturing social and emotional development is to focus on children's distinctive abilities rather than on what may be perceived as their deficits. How might educators' practices make the most of children's assets? How can children's identities be affirmed through everyday relationships, language, and interactions?

The three articles in this part provide teachers with insights and examples of practice that reflect a strengths-based approach to social and emotional development.

In "Promoting Young Children's Social and Emotional Health," **Jeannie Ho** and **Suzanne Funk** describe the foundational importance of social and emotional health and identify specific ways teachers can establish trusting relationships as well as teach, model, and reinforce positive behaviors. With these strategies as priorities, early childhood education settings can be places where happy, engaged children become socially and emotionally healthy.

Vicki S. Collet continues this part's focus on children's strengths in "'I Can Do That!' Fostering Resilience in Young Children." The author describes characteristics of resilience, suggests learning experiences and interactions that will help each child grow in resilience, and identifies characteristics of resilient classrooms.

Children come to school with distinctive experiences and perspectives. In his article, "What About the Children? Teachers Cultivating and Nurturing the Voice and Agency of Young Children," **Brian L. Wright** helps teachers to honor these dimensions of diversity and support the development of each child's individuality and humanity by highlighting activities that help all children know that their actions can make a difference.

REFERENCE

NAEYC. 2022. *Developmentally Appropriate Practice in Early Childhood Programs Serving Children from Birth Through Age 8*. 4th ed. Washington, DC: NAEYC.

Promoting Young Children's Social and Emotional Health

Jeannie Ho and Suzanne Funk

In a preschool classroom, some of the 3- and 4-year-old children smile, laugh, and giggle during free play; are curious about what happens next during story time; ask *what* and *why* questions while doing hands-on activities; and use words to express feelings and needs. In the toy area, Tom and Juan both reach for a small blue car. Tom says, "May I please have it first, then you have it later?" Juan replies, "You have it for five minutes and then I have it for five minutes." Noticing this exchange, their teacher says, "Tom and Juan, you are talking about taking turns. What a great way to play together!"

Tom, Juan, and their classmates are models of social and emotional health in preschool. Children who are socially and emotionally healthy tend to demonstrate, and continue to develop, several important behaviors and skills (adapted from Bilmes 2012 and McClellan & Katz 2001). They

> Are usually in a positive mood

> Listen and follow directions

> Have close relationships with caregivers and peers

> Care about friends and show interest in others

> Recognize, label, and manage their own emotions

> Understand others' emotions and show empathy

> Express wishes and preferences clearly

> Gain access to ongoing play and group activities

> Are able to play, negotiate, and compromise with others

Why Social and Emotional Health Matters

Children's social and emotional health affects their overall development and learning. Research indicates that children who are mentally healthy tend to be happier, show greater motivation to learn, have a more positive attitude toward school, more eagerly participate in class activities, and demonstrate higher academic performance than less mentally healthy peers (Hyson 2004; Kostelnik et al. 2015). Children who exhibit social and emotional difficulties tend to have trouble following directions and participating in learning activities. Compared with healthier peers, they may be more likely to suffer rejection by classmates, have low self-esteem, do poorly in school, and be suspended (Hyson 2004; Kostelnik et al. 2015). Thus, children's social and emotional health is just as important as their physical health, and affects their capacity to develop and potential to lead a fulfilling life.

Teachers can promote children's social and emotional health in many ways, for example, by organizing a material-rich environment to stimulate social interactions among children. This article focuses on two of the most important practices: building trusting relationships and conducting intentional teaching.

Establish Trusting Relationships

Young children develop and learn in the context of relationships. A trusting and caring teacher-child relationship is essential for children's optimum development (Raikes & Edwards 2009). Children who have trusting relationships with their teachers are, on average, more willing to ask questions, solve problems, try new tasks, and express their thinking than their peers without such relationships (O'Connor & McCartney 2007). In her work supervising student teachers, Ho (the first author) often sees children developing positive social and emotional health as a result of close relationships with their teachers. For example, children learn to use words to express their feelings—such as Amy saying to Emily, "I am sad when you use hurting words!"—and to show empathy—as when Arjun gently pats Brian's head and says, "Are you okay? Do you want to hold the teddy bear?"

Children benefit socially, emotionally, and academically when teachers intentionally create close, trusting relationships (Palermo et al. 2007). But gaining the trust of every child is not as simple as being nice and engaging. How can teachers create trusting relationships with all of the children? Consistently offering warmth, affection, respect, and caring is essential.

Showing Warmth and Affection Consistently

Warmth and affection—even on bad days and when children are misbehaving—are critical to children's well-being in early education settings (Ostrosky & Jung 2005). They contribute to developing secure relationships between children and adults, provide models of gentle behavior, and are linked with children's ability to interact positively with peers (Twardosz 2005). The preschoolers we observed used gentle hands and kind words and positively interacted with peers most of the time. Their social and emotional well-being was nourished by their teachers' warmth and affection, which is shown in the following examples:

> Ms. Johnson displays a pleasant facial expression throughout the day. She smiles when greeting children in the morning, says goodbye in the afternoon, and acknowledges children's appropriate behaviors.

> Mr. Logan uses the appropriate tone of voice at all times. His speech is at normal pitch and volume; his tone is relaxed and soft. Even when he has to redirect a child's behavior, he remains calm and warm to convey that his concern is with the behavior—not the child.

> Ms. Aragon gives appropriate touches when necessary, such as a pat on the back, a handshake, hugs, and brief tickles.

> Ms. Lizama moves physically close to the children and bends or crouches to be at the children's eye level while talking to them.

> Mr. Sharma often uses loving comments to show he cares: "I am so happy to see you this morning!," "I missed you yesterday," "I love seeing your smile!" And he is careful to make such comments to all of the children in his classroom.

Respecting and Caring About Every Child

Showing respect is a key way to connect with children and strengthen positive relationships. It helps children feel more confident and competent to explore and learn (Dombro, Jablon, & Stetson 2020). Ms. Carnes establishes and maintains close personal bonds with every child in her classroom by consistently acting in respectful and caring ways. Specifically, she

> **Listens with full attention and restates what children say (often also seizing the opportunity to expose the children to new vocabulary).** Jason, a 4-year-old, says, "Look, I made a truck with lots of LEGO bricks!" Ms. Carnes replies, "Oh, I see, Jason. You built a truck with dozens of LEGO bricks." Jason adds, "I use this truck to deliver apples and bananas to the grocery store." Ms. Carnes responds, "Using a truck to deliver nutritious fruits to the grocery store is helpful." Listening to children attentively and reflectively enhances their self-worth and confidence. When teachers actively listen to children, they convey that they care about what the children have to say, and the children are more likely to share their thoughts, ideas, feelings, and stories.

> **Accepts and reflects children's feelings.** Frowning, Jasper says to the teacher, "Michael has all the big blocks!" Ms. Carnes responds, "Jasper, you seem upset that there are no more large blocks to build with right now. It is difficult to wait!" Amy says with enthusiasm, "We are about to go outside!" Ms. Carnes answers, "The sparkles in your eyes tell me you can hardly wait to go outside. You are excited." When they accept and reflect children's feelings, teachers exhibit sensitivity and caring in a way children understand. Teachers' acknowledgments make children feel heard and accepted (Duffy 2008). As a result, children feel safe to express their emotions—and receive support in identifying, labeling, and better understanding their emotions.

> **Spends private, quality time with individual children through one-on-one activities, such as story reading and game playing.** Emily is sad when her mom leaves. Ms. Carnes reads her a book in a cozy corner with soft pillows and stuffed animals. Afterward, Emily is ready to explore and play in the classroom. Judy complains that no one wants to play with her at the tactile table. Ms. Carnes sits at the table and plays with Judy until another child joins the play. In addition, Ms. Carnes spends quality time with individual children by putting aside other work, moving to the child's level, and conversing openly with the child. Ms. Carnes keeps track to ensure that she speaks with each child regularly, which deepens their relationship and builds trust (Gartrell 2007). Ms. Carnes finds time for these conversations throughout the day, especially during greeting, free play, snack, lunch, and departure time.

Teach Social and Emotional Skills Intentionally

Helping children develop social and emotional skills is the heart and soul of any good program for young children (Gordon & Browne 2014). Teachers (and all caregivers) play key roles in helping children develop social and emotional competence (Kostelnik et al. 2015). Teachers can intentionally support children's social and emotional health by using children's books, planning activities, coaching on the spot, giving effective praise, modeling appropriate behaviors, and providing cues.

Using Children's Books

Reading and discussing children's books is an excellent way to invite children to identify the characters' emotions and relate the characters' experiences to their own (Roberts & Crawford 2008). To introduce a new social or emotional skill, Ms. Coz carefully chooses high-quality books to read aloud at circle time. Sometimes she chooses books related to children's recent social and emotional behaviors in the classroom. When she sees some of the children having trouble sharing toys, she reads aloud *The Rainbow Fish,* by Marcus Pfister. When she finds a child crying because her friend hit her, Ms. Coz reads aloud *Hands Are Not for Hitting,* by Elizabeth Verdick. (For more titles to consider, see "Children's Books for Teaching Social and Emotional Skills.")

Children's Books for Teaching Social and Emotional Skills

Can You Be a Friend?, by Nita Everly

Care Bears Caring Contest, by Nancy Parent, illustrated by David Stein

Fox Makes Friends, by Adam Relf

How Do Dinosaurs Play with Their Friends? by Jane Yolen and Mark Teague

How I Feel Frustrated, by Marcia Leonard

I Can Do It Myself (a Sesame Street Series), by Emily Perl Kingsley, illustrated by Richard Brown

I'm in Charge of Me! by David Parker, illustrated by Sylvia Walker

Mouse Was Mad, by Linda Urban, illustrated by Henry Cole

My Many Colored Days, by Dr. Seuss, illustrated by Steve Johnson and Lou Fancher

Sharing: How Kindness Grows, by Fran Shaw, illustrated by Miki Sakamoto

When I'm Feeling Sad, by Trace Moroney

When Sophie Gets Angry—Really, Really Angry, by Molly Bang

To connect the characters and situations in a book with the children's experiences, Ms. Coz plans to read the book at least twice and also add it to the classroom library. During the second reading, she asks meaningful questions: "What do you think the characters are feeling?," "How would you solve the problem?," "Can you use words from the story to explain how you feel when you . . . ?," "What could we do differently if this happens in our classroom?" These open-ended questions enable children to talk about their own experiences, learn new vocabulary words, and practice social and emotional skills.

Planning Activities

To extend and apply what children learn from reading stories, Ms. Coz plans follow-up activities, such as hands-on crafts, games, and songs. She often uses Book Nook guides, created by the Center on the Social and Emotional Foundations for Early Learning (http://csefel.vanderbilt.edu/resources/strategies.html#booknook). These guides help her embed social and emotional development activities into daily routines, including read-alouds. (For some ideas adapted from Book Nook guides, see "Activities for Supporting Children's Social and Emotional Learning.")

Coaching on the Spot

When they coach children on the spot, teachers help children realize what they are doing, understand how their actions affect others, and choose positive alternatives (Riley et al. 2008). For example, when Ryan and Ethan build a firehouse in the block area, Ethan grabs the fire truck from Ryan, and

Activities for Supporting Children's Social and Emotional Learning

Helping hands chain: Trace and cut out multiple hands for each child. Place them in a pocket or baggie that is easily accessible. As you recognize a child's helping hand behavior, have the child get a hand from their pocket and connect it to the class's helping hand chain. The hands can be placed on the wall to wrap around the room. On a regular basis, celebrate how long the helping hand chain is getting!

Hand puppets: Create character puppets by having children color or paint the pictures, cut them out, and glue them to craft sticks. Once dry, children can bring their puppets to circle time and act out the story while you read the story aloud. Later, they can take the puppets to the story area or puppet center.

Moving to music: Choose songs with lyrics that encourage movement. Before you start, remind the children that they need to listen closely to the words so they know what actions to take. Classic songs like "Head, Shoulders, Knees, and Toes" work well. Many children's CDs have great songs that involve following directions (try "My Ups and Downs" and "Hands Are for Clapping," by Jim Gill). Do the motions with the children as you listen to the songs. After listening to each song several times, children will build confidence and know which motions to do on their own. Point out to the children that they know what to do because they are being such good listeners.

Pass the feeling bag: Place an assortment of scenario picture cards in a bag. As music plays, the children pass the bag. When the music stops, one child picks out a card and identifies it. Have the child talk about how each scenario or item makes him feel and why. Allow children to take turns pulling out picture cards.

Feeling faces collage: Have children cut out different feeling faces from magazines. Mix nontoxic glue and water together in a small bowl. The children put the pictures on top of a piece of paper, take a paintbrush and dip it in glue solution, and paint over their pictures. They can hang their feeling faces collages on the wall.

Share box: Create a special share box that is only introduced during circle time. Children can decorate the box with primary colors or with a bold pattern. Inside the box, place items that can be shared, such as musical instruments, a box of chunky sidewalk chalk, playdough, or several sensory bottles.

Singing: After a story about sharing with friends, sing "Share, share, share your toys; share them with a friend. Share, share, share your toys, let's all play pretend," to the tune of "Row, Row, Row Your Boat." After a story about feelings, sing "If You're Happy and You Know It" with a variety of emotions and body gestures.

(Adapted, with permission, from Book Nook, created by the Center on the Social and Emotional Foundations for Early Learning. To use Book Nook guides at no cost, visit http://csefel.vanderbilt.edu/resources/strategies.html#booknook.)

Ryan cries. Ms. Coz crouches down at Ethan's level to look into his eyes; calmly and warmly, she says, "Ryan was still using the truck. When you took it away from him, he got upset. What could you do to make Ryan feel better?" After Ethan says he is sorry and gives back the fire truck, Ms. Coz says, "Next time if you want to play with the toy Ryan is using, could you ask if he will share?" Ms. Coz follows up by observing Ethan and providing immediate positive feedback on his desirable behavior.

Giving Effective Praise

Meaningful feedback pertinent to the task at hand in the form of effective praise is a powerful strategy for fostering children's social and emotional development (Kostelnik et al. 2015). To make praise effective, teachers describe specifically what they see—without generalizing, evaluating, or making comparisons. When Emily finishes her drawing, Ms. Coz notices her

picture and her smile. Ms. Coz says, "I see a blue sky, a yellow sun, and green grass around the big brown tree. This picture makes you happy, doesn't it?" This praise is effective because Ms. Coz offers detailed, positive comments immediately after desirable behavior occurs. Noticing Ethan asking Ryan politely for a policewoman figure, Ms. Coz says, "Ethan, you used the magic words *May I please?* to ask for that policewoman while you and Ryan were building the firehouse together. Great job!" Smiling, Ethan responds, "We are friends and we can share things."

Modeling Appropriate Behavior

Children learn by observing other people, getting ideas about how new behaviors are formed, and using the ideas to guide their actions (Bandura 1977). Many studies have found that modeling—or demonstrating appropriate behaviors—teaches and enhances children's social and emotional skills (Hyson 2004; Katz & McClellan 1997). This research-based conclusion is evidenced in Ms. Coz's and Ms. Carnes's classes. Both teachers implement several noninvasive strategies—including modeling—that their center administrators created to support teachers in promoting socially and emotionally healthy behaviors. They display the strategies on the classroom wall and put them into action by

> Moving closer to children, when needed, as a nonverbal cue to rethink behaviors

> Modeling appropriate warm and respectful behavior throughout the day and at specific moments when a gentle reminder is needed

> Using nonverbal gestures and contact (e.g., nodding the head, giving thumbs-up signs, and touching children gently on the shoulder) to send messages

> Employing simple language (e.g., "Walking feet, please" and "Use gentle hands") to set expectations and give reminders

> Acknowledging a kind act on the spot or praising a group effort for a job well done

> Placing a hand—gently—on a child's hand to redirect attention and behavior

When children see teachers demonstrate these noninvasive strategies, they often smile, use their gentle hands, say *please* and *thank you*, give hugs and high fives, and use words to express their feelings.

In addition to being role models, the teachers use the children's appropriate behaviors to model social and emotional skills. They carefully observe and record details about how children apply the target skills, and they share their observations with the children through puppet shows during circle time. Using puppets to demonstrate children's appropriate behaviors helps children learn social and emotional skills meaningfully.

Providing Cues

Providing cues to engage children in appropriate social behavior has been shown over time to improve their social behavior with their peers (Bovey & Strain 2005). Ms. Coz and Ms. Carnes often provide verbal cues to help some children participate in activities. Before playtime, for example, Ms. Carnes asks, "James, who are you going to ask to play with you at center time?" During playtime, she suggests, "Saanvi, can you ask Anna to build an airplane with you?" To teach sharing and turn taking, Ms. Coz asks Steven, who has been waiting to play with a toy dolphin for a while, "What magic words could you use to have a turn with the dolphin John is using?"

Both Ms. Coz and Ms. Carnes prominently display visual cues in their classrooms to assist children's social and emotional interactions. For example, they provide teacher-made hand puppets to guide children to use quiet voices, helping hands, and walking feet. To help children calm down, they also created a "push wall"—a designated spot on the wall to push anger out—and use puppets to demonstrate the strategy. These puppets, demonstrations, and explanations are essential for clarifying and modeling appropriate behavior—and the visual cues are essential for reminding the children to practice what they have learned. Long-term visual cues function like a third teacher in the sense that children use the cues to remind one another of solutions and appropriate actions.

Reflection Questions

1. Think about a group of children with whom you work or know well. Do you consider a few of those children to be especially socially and emotionally healthy? What factors may contribute to their well-being?

2. Identify one child with whom you find it challenging to establish a trusting relationship, and plan steps to strengthen that relationship.

3. Relationships are at the heart of developmentally appropriate practice. Refer to the importance of relationships in *Developmentally Appropriate Practice* (NAEYC 2022), specifically pages 112–113 and 123–125, and consider how to apply several key ideas in your own early learning setting.

4. In your experience, do children demonstrate their social and emotional health in different ways? If yes, what factors may influence these differences (e.g., cultural characteristics, family expectations, disabilities)?

5. Choose one of the many teaching strategies described in this article. Implement this strategy, assess its effects, and share the results with a colleague or other partner.

6. Read through the points under the heading "Establishing Respectful, Reciprocal Relationships" on pages 150–151 in *Developmentally Appropriate Practice* (NAEYC 2022). Evaluate which ideas you are familiar with and where you need to develop your knowledge and understanding to better connect with children's families to support children's social and emotional health together.

Conclusion

Teachers and caregivers promote children's social and emotional health by establishing trusting relationships, created when teachers express warmth, affection, and respect. Teachers can intentionally teach and enhance these skills using evidence-based strategies to teach, model, and reinforce positive behaviors. As evidenced in the preschool classrooms we observed, teachers who prioritize developing children's social and emotional health are richly rewarded with happy, engaged children who learn to avoid and resolve conflicts, share and take turns, and express their emotions in productive ways.

REFERENCES

Bandura, A. 1977. *Social Learning Theory.* Englewood Cliffs, NJ: Prentice-Hall.

Bilmes, J. 2012. *Beyond Behavior Management: The Six Life Skills Children Need.* 2nd ed. St. Paul, MN: Redleaf.

Bovey, T., & P. Strain. 2005. "Strategies for Increasing Peer Social Interactions: Prompting and Acknowledgment." Center on the Social and Emotional Foundations for Early Learning. What Works Briefs. http://csefel.vanderbilt.edu/briefs/wwb17.pdf.

Dombro, A.L., J. Jablon, & C. Stetson. 2020. *Powerful Interactions: How to Connect with Children to Extend Their Learning.* 2nd ed. Washington, DC: NAEYC.

Duffy, R. 2008. "Are Feelings Fixable?" *Exchange* 30 (6): 87–90.

Gartrell, D. 2007. *A Guidance Approach for the Encouraging Classroom.* 4th ed. Florence, KY: Thomson Delmar Learning.

Gordon, A.M., & K.W. Browne. 2014. *Beginnings and Beyond: Foundations in Early Childhood Education.* 9th ed. Belmont, CA: Cengage.

Hyson, M. 2004. *The Emotional Development of Young Children: Building an Emotion-Centered Curriculum.* 2nd ed. New York: Teachers College Press.

Katz, L.G., & D.E. McClellan. 1997. *Fostering Children's Social Competence: The Teacher's Role.* Washington, DC: NAEYC.

Kostelnik, M.J., A.K. Soderman, A.P. Whiren, M.L. Rupiper, & K.M. Gregory. 2015. *Guiding Children's Social Development and Learning: Theory and Skills.* 8th ed. Stamford, CT: Cengage.

McClellan, D., & L.G. Katz. 2001. "Assessing Young Children's Social Competence." Champaign, IL: ERIC Clearinghouse on Elementary and Early Childhood Education. http://files.eric.ed.gov/fulltext/ED450953.pdf.

NAEYC. 2022. *Developmentally Appropriate Practice in Early Childhood Programs Serving Children from Birth Through Age 8.* 4th ed. Washington, DC: NAEYC.

O'Connor, E., & K. McCartney. 2007. "Examining Teacher–Child Relationships and Achievement as Part of an Ecological Model of Development." *American Educational Research Journal* 44 (2): 340–69.

Ostrosky, M.M., & E.Y. Jung. 2005. "Building Positive Teacher–Child Relationships." Center on the Social and Emotional Foundations for Early Learning. What Works Briefs. http://csefel.vanderbilt.edu/briefs/wwb12.pdf.

Palermo, F., L.D. Hanish, C.L. Martin, R.A. Fabes, & M. Reiser. 2007. "Preschoolers' Academic Readiness: What Role Does the Teacher–Child Relationship Play?" *Early Childhood Research Quarterly* 22 (4): 407–22. www.ncbi.nlm.nih.gov/pmc/articles/PMC3856866.

Raikes, H.H., & C.P. Edwards. 2009. *Extending the Dance in Infant and Toddler Caregiving: Enhancing Attachment and Relationships.* Baltimore: Brookes.

Riley, D., R.R. San Juan, J. Klinkner, & A. Ramminger. 2008. *Social and Emotional Development: Connecting Science and Practice in Early Childhood Settings.* St. Paul, MN: Redleaf; Washington, DC: NAEYC.

Roberts, S.K., & P.A. Crawford. 2008. "Real Life Calls for Real Books: Literature to Help Children Cope with Family Stressors." *Young Children* 63 (5): 12–17.

Twardosz, S. 2005. "Expressing Warmth and Affection to Children." Center on the Social and Emotional Foundations for Early Learning. What Works Briefs. http://csefel.vanderbilt.edu/briefs/wwb20.pdf.

About the Authors

Jeannie Ho, EdD, is a professor at Montgomery College, in Rockville, Maryland, where she teaches courses in early childhood education. Her research focus is effective teaching practices and children's social and emotional development.

Suzanne Funk, MSEd, is the former director of Geneva Day School, located in Potomac, Maryland, and a former adjunct professor in early childhood education at Montgomery College. She has worked with local child center directors to enhance the quality of services available for all young children. She is now retired from the education profession with over 50 years of experience in federal, state, and local agencies.

"I Can Do That!"

Fostering Resilience in Young Children

Vicki S. Collet

Mrs. Durkin's kindergarten classroom is full of busy learners. Klaus makes a birthday card for his classmate, saying the words aloud, stretching out the sounds as he writes. Santos is at the SmartBoard and the audio is not working; he turns the volume knob, but no sound is emitted. Next, he removes and then reinserts the audio cord, smiling as the music begins playing. Gracie reads aloud carefully, noticing when she makes a mistake and stopping to reread and correct herself. By responding proactively when confronted with problems during learning, these students are exhibiting resilience. Their actions match their language, as Mrs. Durkin has taught them to say and feel "I can do that!"

Classrooms that foster resilience often share a key feature: children are not afraid to make mistakes (Martin & Marsh 2008). There is a strong culture of inquiry and an atmosphere reflecting a willingness to engage in trial and error. Because learning requires experimenting and facing unknowns, fostering resilience with a flexible, buoyant classroom environment enhances students' growth.

Resilient students understand that changes and challenges bring opportunities. They view mistakes as a chance to learn, accepting that failing often precedes succeeding (Seligman 2007) and recognizing that effort develops knowledge and skill. Rather than believing that success depends solely or even primarily on innate talent, they recognize that success largely depends on effort (Dweck 2002). Resilient children see difficulties as temporary setbacks; they focus on what they can do.

In contrast, children who are less resilient tend to see failure as permanent, pervasive, and out of their control (Seligman 2011). Such students usually fear making mistakes, which they associate with humiliation or disappointment (Goldstein & Brooks 2013). Because of this fear, they may choose what to do in the classroom based on how successful they think they will be. If they do not feel certain that they will succeed, they might avoid—rather than embrace—challenges. During class, children who are less resilient might not participate because they worry about what others will think if they give an incorrect answer. Viewing their performance as a measure of their value and potential, they may choose to forgo a learning opportunity rather than risk being embarrassed.

Teachers can help students overcome their fears, tackle challenges, and increase resilience. Learning experiences that build resilience create opportunities for students to correct errors and build understanding. Teachers can set the stage for resilience as they design the physical space of the classroom and plan for instruction.

What Is Resilience?

Some educators may use different terms (e.g., persistence, flexibility) to describe the set of qualities that this article labels as resilience. The American Psychological Association (n.d.) provides a helpful definition and perspective:

> Resilience is the process of adapting well in the face of adversity. Resilience is not a trait that people either have or do not have. It involves behaviors, thoughts, and actions that can be learned and developed in anyone.

Nurturing this trait at an early age is crucial to building lifelong learners.

Learning Experiences that Increase Resilience

Let's return to Mrs. Durkin's kindergarten classroom, where she planned reading and writing instruction that builds resilience along with literacy. Mrs. Durkin's resilient environment had an array of components, ranging from providing resources to emphasizing the learning process.

"I Can Do That!" Fostering Resilience in Young Children

17

Providing Resources

Collaboratively creating and encouraging students to use classroom resources, such as process charts, word walls, and letter-sound cards, engenders problem-solving attitudes. For example, a chart created by Mrs. Durkin's class, "Help for Writing," included a list (with accompanying visuals) of resources for writing: ask a friend, word wall, letter cards, My Word Bank (each child's file box of words), posters, and finally, Mrs. Durkin. Although Mrs. Durkin's name had originally appeared at the top of the list, after the class brainstormed so many other resources, they decided together that they could move her to the bottom of the list!

Helping Children Set Goals

Having children set short-term goals is another avenue for increasing resilience. When teachers provide the support students need to develop and achieve these goals, they help students recognize that success requires effort and is incremental. In Mrs. Durkin's room, students set personal goals about how much writing they would do. Allison showed growth toward this goal. Early in the school year, Allison's narratives focused on her drawings, to which she had added just a few words. Over time, her writing stamina increased, and she was pleased when her stories filled the whole page. This experience helped her see the connection between effort and outcome in achieving aspirations. Resilient children believe that they can attain their personal goals (Zolkoski & Bullock 2012).

Valuing Effort

When teachers value children's efforts, they foster resilience. In Mrs. Durkin's classroom, making an attempt was prized over perfection. When students wrote, for example, they were encouraged to include the sounds they heard in a word so they could express their ideas using words that they had not yet learned to spell. At the same time, to help children gradually become both expressive and accurate writers, Mrs. Durkin also provided letter-sound cards and supported students in using them. Although she had made these cards available from the beginning of the year, Mrs. Durkin highlighted the features of the cards (e.g., picture, letter, and other possible spellings) throughout the year to draw students' attention to how the cards might be used during reading and writing.

This combination of providing resources and valuing effort over perfection allowed Siobhán to unabashedly include the word *nomony* (pneumonia) in her writing at the zoo center (see left). While Siobhán was a long way from learning

Books that Help Build Resiliency in Children Ages 5 to 8

Amazing Grace

By Mary Hoffman, illustrated by Caroline Binch (1991)

Although a classmate tells Grace that she cannot play Peter Pan in the school play because she is black, Grace discovers that she can do anything she sets her mind to.

Bully

By Laura Vaccaro Seeger (2013)

A little bull discovers that he has been a big bully.

DeShawn Days

By Tony Medina, illustrated by R. Gregory Christie (2001)

In this uplifting story told in verse, a young boy living in the inner city projects tells about his hopes, fears, and dreams.

Fred Stays with Me!

By Nancy Coffelt, illustrated by Tricia Tusa (2007)

A child describes how she lives sometimes with her mother and sometimes with her father, but her dog is her constant companion.

The Matchbox Diary/El diario de las cajas de fósforos

By Paul Fleischman, illustrated by Bagram Ibatoulline (2013)

Follow a girl's perusal of her great-grandfather's collection of matchboxes holding mementos that document his journey from Italy to a new country.

Monday, Wednesday, and Every Other Weekend

By Karen Stanton (2014)

Although Henry enjoys the time he spends at his mother's apartment and his father's house, his dog, Pomegranate, gets confused about which place is home.

The Money We'll Save

By Brock Cole (2011)

In nineteenth-century New York City, when Pa brings home a young turkey in hopes of saving money on their Christmas dinner, his family faces all sorts of trouble and expense in their tiny apartment.

My Name Is Sangoel

By Karen Lynn Williams and Khadra Mohammed, illustrated by Catherine Stock (2009)

As a refugee from Sudan, Sangoel is frustrated that no one in the United States can pronounce his name correctly until he finds a clever way to solve the problem.

My Name Is Yoon

By Helen Recorvits, illustrated by Gabi Swiatkowska (2003)

Disliking the way her name looks written in English, Korean-born Yoon, or "shining wisdom," tries out different names ("Cat," "Bird," and "Cupcake") to feel more comfortable in her new school and new country.

Oliver Finds His Way

By Phyllis Root, illustrated by Christopher Denise (2002)

Oliver the bear becomes lost when he chases a leaf to the edge of the woods, but then he comes up with an idea to find his way back home.

Otto the Book Bear/Otto: El oso de libro

By Katie Cleminson (2012)

Otto lives in a book in a house, but when no one is looking he comes to life. He reads his favorite stories and practices his writing, until he is left behind and must set out in search of a new home.

Tap Tap Boom Boom

By Elizabeth Bluemle, illustrated by G. Brian Karas (2014)

"It's a mad dash for shelter as rain sweeps into an urban neighborhood. Where to go? The subway! It's the perfect place to wait out the wind and weather. Strangers share smiles and umbrellas and take delight in the experience of a city thunderstorm." (From the dust jacket)

These Hands

By Margaret H. Mason, illustrated by Floyd Cooper (2010)

An African American man tells his grandson about a time when, despite all the wonderful things his hands could do, they could not touch bread at the Wonder Bread factory. Based on stories of bakery union workers, the book includes historical notes.

(From Lacina, Baumi, & Taylor 2016)

Note: Summaries were obtained from the Library of Congress unless otherwise indicated

Self-Assessment Rubric

4.

I gave my best effort and worked the whole time.

3.

I gave my best effort and worked most of the time.

2.

I worked a little, but I talked and played a lot. I didn't get finished.

1.

I didn't work, and I played the whole time.

to correctly spell *pneumonia*, her effort to express a complex topic in writing was an accomplishment—from Mrs. Durkin and Siobhán herself. To nurture the students' resilience, Mrs. Durkin encouraged the students to self-assess their efforts, using rubrics such as the one pictured (left). Whether assessment is formal or informal, how children's work is received affects how they feel about their efforts and their likelihood of embracing challenges in the future. (For more on beneficial praise, see "Praise that Fosters Resilience" on page 22.) Emphasizing effort over product enhances students' resilience.

Offering Strategies

Teaching children strategies that build resilience gives them tools to tackle learning tasks and subtly reinforces the message that learning takes effort. For example, students who struggle as they learn to read often look to the teacher whenever they come to an unknown word. Teachers foster resilience when, instead of supplying the word right away, they encourage application of a strategy or use of a resource, such as rereading, applying context clues, considering previous experiences, or using sound/symbol associations (like the letter-sound cards described earlier). Mrs. Durkin quickly responded to Scarlett's upward glance for assistance with an unknown word by pointing back to the book, redirecting Scarlett's attention to cues that she had and skills she could use. If teachers mindfully take this approach, they build their students' independence and resilience. But *mindfully* is key: Teachers should adjust the level of support so that it leads to student success.

FAMILY ENGAGEMENT

At home, interactions with parents and other caregivers can help children develop resilience and learn to deal well with challenges. Families can be both coaches and cheerleaders by recognizing their children's strengths and supporting them during difficult experiences. Share the following information and suggestions with families.

> **Encourage your child to try something even if it seems hard.** Media and peers tend to emphasize talent and performance over effort and persistence, which can foster fear of failure and cause children to avoid risks or procrastinate when they do not feel confident. Although you may be inclined to shield your child from difficult situations, early experiences with failure and disappointment, when accompanied by your support and reassurance, will help your child develop lifelong attributes of persistence and confidence. Learning how to cope with setbacks and discouragement develops the ability to bounce back from adversity. Rather than avoid struggle, resilient people see it as an opportunity or challenge.

> **Define failure and mistakes as temporary and valuable opportunities to learn.** Your attitudes toward and responses to failure and mistakes—whether your own or your child's—influence how your child responds and the degree of resilience he will develop. Patience is key! When your child makes a mistake, respond with understanding and encouragement rather than blame or criticism. If a household chore, like making the bed, is not done properly, don't just redo it yourself—model and describe the process and support your child as his competence with the task increases. Taking this approach not only helps children see success as an outcome of effort but also encourages them to be less afraid of making mistakes and more willing to persist.

> **When your child faces a difficult situation, don't solve the problem for her.** Instead, help her analyze what happened and why, and encourage her to identify a solution to try. Your questions can guide the problem-solving process. Listen and be encouraging as your child develops the ability to find solutions.

> **Offer your child small decisions early and often.** Doing so will help him learn about cause and effect and prepare him for making more consequential decisions later. Even toddlers can have a say in what clothes they wear or whether to have a story before or after bath time. Seeing the effects of their own choices gives them a sense of control.

> **Be mindful of what you praise your child for.** Although comments like "You are so smart!" may come naturally, praising a child's efforts ("You worked so hard! Look what you've accomplished!") helps them see the connection between persistence and outcome. Valuing effort also helps children focus on personal responsibility and factors that are in their control instead of outside of it—an essential part of resiliency.

Life is challenging and ever changing, but support from parents and caregivers can equip children to face the challenges and changes with confidence!

"I Can Do That!" Fostering Resilience in Young Children

21

Note that Mrs. Durkin did not expect her kindergartners to invent strategies for overcoming their reading challenges—she taught them. During small group reading instruction, for instance, Mrs. Durkin taught a set of strategies to develop the children's persistence in meaning making (Collet 2007). She used an object to introduce and help students remember each strategy: a stop sign to pause and think, a paper clip to make connections, a parrot figure to reread, and a light switch to read on. Later, when children got stuck, they grabbed the corresponding object as a visual reminder of the strategy they had decided to use. In addition, the object gave Mrs. Durkin a way to track which children were having trouble and where to start if she needed to offer extra support. When educators teach and remind students of strategies, students soon use them independently.

Praise that Fosters Resilience

A great way for teachers to inspire resilience is to offer specific praise focused on students' efforts. Praising children for hard work, rather than for their perceived ability, leads them to value learning opportunities and persist in their efforts (Dweck 2010). Students whose efforts are acknowledged want to "immerse themselves in information that could teach them more" (Dweck 2002, 49). As long as the feedback is genuine (i.e., a student really did try hard), children recognize that improvement is related to effort, so they rise to challenges in ways that enhance their knowledge, skills, and resilience.

Mrs. Durkin praised students in ways that valued their efforts and reinforced essential aspects of their learning, such as adding details and sequencing adverbs to their writing. When Jimarcus read the story he wrote about the zoo to Mrs. Durkin, she responded, "Great detail! You told me the giraffe was yellow and the lizard was green. You also used the word *finally*, which let me know that you were almost finished."

Similarly, when Zach read Mrs. Durkin his draft, she said, "Good writing, Zach—very nice! I love how you included a zoo train in your story. I know that you are very interested in trains" (Collet 2011). In those few short words, she expressed high expectations, praised Zach's use of detail, and made a personal connection by recalling Zach's passion for trains. This type of feedback encourages students to learn new things, persist after difficulty, use better strategies for correcting mistakes, and improve performance (Cimpian et al. 2007; Zentall & Morris 2010).

Emphasizing the Learning Process

Emphasizing process enables teachers—and children—to tie together all of the components of resilient classrooms discussed previously. A strong process encompasses appropriate resources, goal setting, effort, and student-centered strategies.

In Mrs. Durkin's classroom, writing workshop time provided opportunities for drafting and revision that cultivated a realistic understanding of the writing process and supported resilience. Like professional writers, students revisited their favorite pieces, improving their writing as they acquired new strategies. They delighted in learning about the caret symbol (^), which they would use to insert new ideas without having to rewrite their whole text. A look through children's writing folders showed that they were taking advantage of it often to add new thoughts to their writing. Correction tape was another favorite tool in Mrs. Durkin's classroom. In contrast to recopying their work to make a correction, which was laborious, using correction tape made the improvement process fun. Tools like these dramatically reduce the consequences of making a mistake, so they help students focus on accomplishing their goals through sustained effort. By offering experiences that emphasize the learning process and encourage risk taking over perfection, teachers create a classroom climate that builds resilience.

Classroom Management Practices that Enhance Resilience

Keeping resilience in mind when creating resources and planning for instruction lays the groundwork for nurturing buoyant learning attitudes. Classroom management is equally important, as it offers opportunities throughout the day to teach appropriate behavior, foster independence, and reinforce a resilient approach to learning.

Managing Behavior

Children benefit from experiencing consistent expectations, rules, and consequences. Seeing the connection between actions and results gives children a sense of predictability and control over their environment—necessary ingredients for resilience. When teachers select logical consequences for

Creating a Resilient Classroom

Instead of doing this . . .	Do this . . .	And get students who . . .
Emphasizing high-stakes assessments	Have students set and work toward short-term goals	See growth as incremental and attainable
Talking about failures or successes as being connected to talent or traits (e.g., "You're so smart!")	Define failure as an opportunity to learn and success as a result of hard work	Are persistent
Requiring correct spelling from emergent writers	Encourage use of invented spelling	Are willing to take risks
Supplying an unknown word when students are reading or writing	Use cues and classroom resources	Recognize their problem-solving skills
Explaining the meaning of texts	Teach comprehension strategies	Value their own thinking and use strategies to figure things out on their own
Providing extensive feedback on final products	Provide feedback throughout the writing process	Value revision and continual improvement
Giving mostly correction	Give encouragement that celebrates steps in the right direction	Feel encouraged, worthwhile, and empowered to persist in their efforts
Praising only outcomes	Acknowledge and support effort, regardless of outcome	Are willing to take on challenges
Applying consequences unrelated to the misbehavior	Set logical, reasonable consequences that are related to the behavior	Learn that choices have consequences and, therefore, better evaluate their future decisions
Performing classroom procedures yourself	Involve students in managing classroom procedures	Feel empowered

inappropriate behavior, children better understand the cause-and-effect relationships that their actions initiate. For example, a young student who colors on his chair would benefit from a warm but firm explanation of where to color and the logical consequence of having to clean his chair. In Mrs. Durkin's room, when children became too noisy while talking to their partners, Mrs. Durkin gave the students a cue by lowering the volume of her own voice when she introduced the next topic for discussion. This emphasized the consequences of students' conduct rather than escalating the concern, and students responded by using the quiet "12-inch voices" that Mrs. Durkin had taught them, which should only be able to be heard a foot away. Through many similar interactions, children gradually recognize the connection between their actions and the consequences that follow, which develops their self-efficacy and internal locus of control—attributes that encourage resilience (Schwarzer & Warner 2013).

Reflection Questions

1. Think about an experience where you learned from making mistakes or failing. What helped you emerge from the situation in a resilient way? How could you incorporate these factors into your classroom environment, taking into account the children's ages and developmental characteristics?

2. Learning requires risk taking and mistakes. What can you do to encourage and celebrate trial and error in your classroom while still protecting children's physical and psychological safety?

3. What resources in your classroom support children's independent problem solving? What additional resources could you incorporate? Review the discussion of various learning formats to enhance learning on pages 187–188 in *Developmentally Appropriate Practice* (NAEYC 2022) for some ideas.

4. When children set and achieve goals, their resilience increases. Are the children you teach setting individual short-term goals? How do you see and encourage appropriate goal setting in children? How do you help children notice and keep track of their progress? How do you adapt your approach to their ages and developmental characteristics?

5. As you work with children, be aware of how you use praise. Are you praising ability or effort? How could you change your wording to focus on effort and encourage persistence? Try out some new wording with a colleague or other partner. For examples of strategies to encourage effort and independence, see page 201 of *Developmentally Appropriate Practice* (NAEYC 2022).

Sharing Responsibilities

Sharing responsibilities with children is another way to promote resilience. Teachers can create meaningful ways to empower children. In Mrs. Durkin's room, there were multiple roles for students to fill each week: the "stick puller" pulled Popsicle sticks with children's names from a basket to determine who would respond to questions; the "table managers" ensured that all students in their group had the necessary items for an activity; and the "light monitor" decided whether lights needed to be on or off for best viewing, depending on the activity. For kindergartners, these are meaningful roles that significantly impact the learning environment. When children see that they are important members of the classroom community, their resilience increases (Henderson 2012).

Conclusion

Through their instruction, resources, responses to students, and management procedures, teachers can present problems as opportunities awaiting creative solutions. When children learn to handle, rather than avoid, less-than-ideal situations in the classroom, they build resilience that can transfer beyond the classroom walls. Difficult experiences provide children with opportunities to show determination, using available resources to rise above disappointment. When problems arise, resilient children don't blame others or themselves; their energy is focused on solutions, asking, "What can I do differently?"

As teachers build students' resilience, students come to recognize mistakes and failures as chances to learn; they realize that discovery requires trying the unfamiliar. (For specific classroom practices and general approaches that can be modified to nurture resilience, see "Creating a Resilient Classroom" on page 23.) Developing resilience is an important step toward becoming a lifelong learner who seeks challenges and uses mistakes as stepping stones to personal and academic success.

REFERENCES

American Psychological Association. n.d. "What Is Resilience?" *The Road to Resilience.* www.apa.org/helpcenter/road-resilience.aspx.

Cimpian, A., H.-M.C. Arce, E.M. Markman, & C.S. Dweck. 2007. "Subtle Linguistic Cues Affect Children's Motivation." *Psychological Science* 18 (4): 314–16.

Collet, V.S. 2007. "Fix-Up Tools: Strategies for Clarifying Comprehension." *Colorado Reading Council Journal* (Fall): 31–34.

Collet, V.S. 2011. "The Gradual Increase of Responsibility: Scaffolds for Change." ProQuest Dissertations and Theses database. (UMI Number: 3475305).

Dweck, C.S. 2002. "Messages That Motivate: How Praise Molds Students' Beliefs, Motivation, and Performance (in Surprising Ways)." In *Improving Academic Achievement: Impact of Psychological Factors on Education,* ed. J. Aronson, 37–59. San Diego, CA: Academic Press.

Dweck, C.S. 2010. "Mind-Sets and Equitable Education." *Principal Leadership* 10 (5): 26–29.

Goldstein, S., & R.B. Brooks, eds. 2013. *Handbook of Resilience in Children.* 2nd ed. New York: Springer.

Henderson, N. 2012. "Resilience in Schools and Curriculum Design." In *The Social Ecology of Resilience: A Handbook of Theory and Practice,* ed. M. Ungar, 297–306. New York: Springer.

Lacina, J., M. Baumi, & E.R. Taylor. 2016. "Promoting Resilience Through Read-Alouds." *Young Children* 71 (2): 16–21.

Martin, A.J., & H.W. Marsh. 2008. "Academic Buoyancy: Towards an Understanding of Students' Everyday Academic Resilience." *Journal of School Psychology* 46 (1): 53–83.

NAEYC. 2022. *Developmentally Appropriate Practice in Early Childhood Programs Serving Children from Birth Through Age 8.* 4th ed. Washington, DC: NAEYC.

Seligman, M.E.P. 2007. *The Optimistic Child: A Proven Program to Safeguard Children Against Depression and Build Lifelong Resilience.* New York: Houghton Mifflin.

Seligman, M.E.P. 2011. "Building Resilience." *Harvard Business Review* 89 (Apr.): 100–106.

Schwarzer, R., & L.M. Warner. 2013. "Perceived Self-Efficacy and Its Relationship to Resilience." In *Resilience in Children, Adolescents, and Adults,* eds. S. Prince-Embury & D.H. Saklofske, 139–50. New York: Springer.

Zentall, S.R., & B.J. Morris. 2010. "'Good Job, You're So Smart': The Effects of Inconsistency of Praise Type on Young Children's Motivation." *Journal of Experimental Psychology* 107 (2): 155–63.

Zolkoski, S.M., & L.M. Bullock. 2012. "Resilience in Children and Youth: A Review." *Children and Youth Services Review* 34 (12): 2295–2303.

About the Author

Vicki S. Collet, PhD, is associate professor of childhood education and associate director of the Northwest Arkansas Writing Project at the University of Arkansas. Vicki has taught and coached in early childhood classrooms and worked on district and state literacy initiatives.

Photographs: p. 16, © Getty Images; pp. 18, 20 (both), courtesy of the author

"I Can Do That!" Fostering Resilience in Young Children

25

What About the Children?

Teachers Cultivating and Nurturing the Voice and Agency of Young Children

Brian L. Wright

What about the children?

To ignore is so easy

—Yolanda Adams, "What About the Children?"

This lyric from the chorus of gospel singer Yolanda Adams's "What About the Children?" captures the critical need for early childhood educators to listen to the insights of and pay close attention to the experiences, perspectives, and realities of *all* children. This need is conveyed further by the phrase "to ignore is so easy," especially given the reality that childhoods are unequal along lines of race, class, gender, language, ability, and disability. Therefore, children from marginalized groups often receive an education that does not recognize their worth, agency, potential, and brilliance (Wright with Counsell 2018).

Guided by this reality, the critical need for early childhood educators to be culturally competent in recognizing what children learn in their homes and communities as relevant to in-school learning is the focus of this article. Teachers' knowledge and understanding of the links between race, culture, and learning are vital to effectively cultivating and nurturing voice and agency in young children. Understanding how race and culture matter for learning manifests in bold and honest conversations and the delivery of creative lessons and activities in which teachers encourage children to explore their racial, ethnic, and cultural differences. Encouraging young children to share their perspectives, experiences, and realities based on their cultural worlds of home, school, and community provides opportunities to cultivate and nurture their voices and agency toward advancing equity in early childhood education. In the sections that follow, there is a discussion of the impact of inequitable schooling on children of color in general and Black children, particularly Black boys. Then, the focus is on children's awareness of racial differences and why the silence about these matters allows children to draw their own often misguided conclusions. The article concludes with an explanation of why it is necessary to cultivate and nurture voice and agency in young children through meaningful activities and authentic multicultural children's books.

Schools as Sites of Inequality

Inequitable schooling contributes in substantive ways to missed essential opportunities to cultivate and nurture the ideas, interests, strengths, and abilities of children from culturally, linguistically, and economically diverse backgrounds. An example of inequitable schooling is the way in which Black boys—as early as preschool—are frequently viewed by White educators as older and less innocent than their White peers, a practice called *adultification*. Additionally, their play is perceived as more dangerous, violent, and not developmentally appropriate (Wright with Counsell 2018; Wright 2019).

According to a 2014 report from the US Department of Education's Office for Civil Rights, Black children make up 18 percent of preschool enrollment, but they represent 48 percent of preschool children receiving one or more out-of-school suspensions (OCR 2014). In comparison, White children represent 41 percent of preschool enrollment but only 28 percent of preschool children receiving one or more out-of-school suspensions. These data are telling and are a clarion call for positive changes in schools and classrooms related to race, diversity, equity, and inclusion. The lack of familiarity by educators to recognize the diverse ways that children organize their experiences and express meaning undermines children's sense of belonging, becoming, and being. This, in turn, places the self-identity, voice, and agency of Black boys and other marginalized children in jeopardy. Further, these deficit approaches create a clash between children of color and their languages, literacies, and cultural ways of being as deficiencies to be overcome in learning and, by extension, legitimize dominant language, literacy, and cultural ways of schooling as the sole gatekeepers to school success. Such a belief not only raises the question *What about the children?*, but, more specifically, *What about the languages and other cultural practices that children of color bring to the early childhood education classroom?* Moreover, these questions are a reminder of why early childhood educators must be culturally competent about matters of race, diversity, equity, and inclusion.

They're Not Too Young to Talk About Race

It is a mistake to assume that young children are unaware of racial differences and that they do not discriminate based on race, class, and gender. It is well documented (Kuh et al. 2016; Ramsey 2015; Souto-Manning 2013) that children quickly learn from their environment to attach beliefs, attitudes, and values to differences and to mimic dominant society's discriminatory practices unless such biases and behaviors are challenged using anti-bias and anti-racist teachings (Derman-Sparks & Edwards with Goins 2020; Kendi 2019). Comments and interactions that children notice as well as their curiosity about racial and cultural differences cannot be ignored. Children want to know more about the world in which they live. Teachers, therefore, must be culturally competent and astute in their observations of young children to understand and accurately interpret their sense-making practices to cultivate, nurture, and recognize each child's individuality and humanity in ways that develop their voice and agency. This is especially true for teachers working with children marginalized by systems of inequality (Blackburn 2014).

In the remainder of this article, I describe two activities that teachers can use to facilitate the development of voice and agency in all children. These activities build on children's strengths and interests and go beyond the contributions level (surface-level topics) of food, fun, fashion, and folklore (Banks 1994, 2014; Ford et al. 2017). These activities are grounded in the following:

1. Children notice and think about racial differences, and they engage (perhaps unwittingly) in discriminatory practices based on race, class, gender, and other characteristics.

2. When adults allow children to draw their own conclusions based on what they see, hear, and read without critical and courageous conversations, racism and discrimination are reinforced.

3. Early childhood educators play an important role in helping children develop positive attitudes, individual voice, and personal agency to promote a more just future.

An Activity to Cultivate and Nurture Voice

One activity to cultivate and nurture voice in young children is centered around a poem by George Ella Lyon, "Where I'm From." To engage children in this activity, the teacher reads aloud the poem as the children read silently. The teacher draws attention to the author of the poem's inclusion of specific details representing culture and ethnicity (e.g., food, family names, location). Children are given several options to represent their version of the poem to capture their cultural and personal identities. This poem invites children and their families' experiences and histories into the early childhood classroom. The poem follows a repeating pattern ("I am from . . .") that recalls details, evokes memories, and has the potential to encourage some excellent poetry writing by young children (Christensen 1997/1998). The power of this poem is its ability to bring together the individual and collective voices within the classroom.

As children work on their poems, teachers should encourage them to include aspects related to their cultural wealth, such as their home country or native language, the history of their name or names of family members (e.g., aunts, uncles, cousins), favorite dishes served during family gatherings, special places they go with their family, and more. As mentioned above, teachers should provide children with different options to choose from to represent their personal "Where I'm From" poems. For example, children can create a Me Poster that includes, but is not limited to, family photos, pictures from old

magazines, and other cultural artifacts that represent and reflect the child's cultural and personal identity, family, and community. Or, children might create a diorama using a shoebox to represent different aspects of their cultural identity, family, and community. Children can also create a skit to dramatize an element of their culture or an illustrated poem that shows the beauty of their culture through color. Additionally, teachers should encourage bilingual children to choose the language(s) in which they wish to compose their poem. Teachers can invite children to share with their peers in either large or small group settings.

An Activity to Cultivate and Nurture Agency

Agency answers the questions *What actions can I take?* and *Will my actions make a difference?* Agency is children's ability to construct and co-construct their environment by negotiating different courses of action. For example, when children choose among different learning center activities or negotiate sharing props during dramatic play, they exercise agency by problem solving to satisfy both individual and group needs (Wright with Counsell 2018; Wright, Counsell, & Tate 2015).

Cultivating agency in young children requires the delivery of curriculum and instruction that encourages children to be actively involved in their own learning by asking questions, sharing insights, and providing opinions. Fostering agency in young children provides opportunities to build a child-centered and child-driven learning environment where multiple and opposing points of view, empowerment, equity, and social justice are at the center of recognizing each child's strengths and talents.

Authentic multicultural children's books serve as a developmentally appropriate way to cultivate and nurture agency in young children. They can introduce children to a variety of topics such as cultural pride, self-identity, gender expression, friendships, families, and much more. All children, but especially children of color, need what Rudine Sims Bishop (1990) calls "mirror" books—that is, books that reflect themselves, their families, and their communities in positive ways. Currently there are far more "window" books—books that give a glimpse into the lives of other people (mainly in the White world)—

than mirror books showing children of color their own communities. These mirror books highlight cultural histories, music, the arts, language varieties, fashion, cuisine, and other culturally rich experiences found in communities of color but not always found in school curricula.

Here is a list of picture books featuring topics that children from diverse cultural and linguistic backgrounds might see in their everyday lives and ways teachers can use them to cultivate and nurture children's agency and voice:

> *Hats of Faith,* by Medeia Cohan, exposes children to people around the world who share in the practice of covering their heads for similar and different reasons. Moreover, this book helps educate and prepare young children for a culturally diverse world in which they take a stand for inclusivity. Teachers can invite children to investigate the concrete, behavioral, and symbolic purposes of the head coverings that most interest them.

> *Hey Black Child,* by Useni Eugene Perkins, uses words and visuals to introduce readers to important people and events from Black American history. It encourages Black children to pursue their dreams and, by extension, all children to take pride in their cultural backgrounds.

> *Pancho Rabbit and the Coyote: A Migrant's Tale,* by Duncan Tonatiuh, uses an allegorical tale to discuss the hardships faced by thousands of families who illegally cross the border to make a better life for themselves and their children.

> *Pink Is for Boys,* by Robb Pearlman, challenges the gender stereotype that pink and purple are feminine colors. The author invites children to celebrate all the colors of the rainbow. Teachers can design their own celebration of the colors of the world and encourage each child to share how these colors enrich the world.

> *René Has Two Last Names/Rene tiene dos apellidos,* by René Colato-Laínez, is a bilingual book that describes a young boy's cultural pride when he uses the last names of both his mother's and father's families—an important Latino/a tradition.

When early childhood educators provide children with books that are mirrors and windows (Bishop 1990), children develop pride in their cultural and linguistic identity. They notice similarities and differences. These observations become conversation starters for rich dialogue based on children's insights, questions, and experiences.

Conclusion

It is a mistake to assume that young children are too young to utilize their voice and agency to develop deeper and richer learning experiences as well as take a stand for equity and social justice. Giving rise to children's voices in this way reaches far beyond their individual experiences and instead empowers them through agency to think about the experiences of others. When early childhood educators recognize that all children have a right to freedom of expression and the right to be heard, then questions about the children are not so easily ignored.

REFERENCES

Banks, J.A. 1994. *Multiethnic Education: Theory and Practice.* 3rd ed. Boston: Allyn & Bacon.

Banks, J.A. 2014. *An Introduction to Multicultural Education.* 5th ed. New York: Pearson.

Bishop, R.S. 1990. "Mirrors, Windows, and Sliding Glass Doors." *Perspectives: Choosing and Using Books for the Classroom* 6 (3): ix–xi.

Blackburn, M.V. 2014. "Humanizing Research with LGBTQ Youth Through Dialogic Communication, Consciousness Raising, and Action." In *Humanizing Research: Decolonizing Qualitative Inquiry with Youth and Communities,* eds. D. Paris & M.T. Winn, 43–57. Thousand Oaks, CA: SAGE Publications.

Christensen, L. 1997/1998. "Where I'm From: Inviting Student Lives into the Classroom." *Rethinking Schools* 12 (2): 392–395.

Derman-Sparks, L., & J.O. Edwards. With C.M. Goins. 2020. *Anti-Bias Education for Young Children and Ourselves.* 2nd ed. Washington, DC: NAEYC.

Ford, D.Y., B.L. Wright, T.C. Grantham, & J.L. Moore III. 2017. "Infusing Culture and Equity in Gifted Education for Students of Color: Three Frameworks." In *From Giftedness to Gifted Education: Reflecting Theory in Practice,* eds. J. Plucker, A. Rinn-McCann, & M. Makel, 183–201. Waco, TX: Prufrock Press.

Brian L. Wright has been bringing his expertise to the NAEYC community both as a writer and a consulting editor since 2015. The following is a list of his NAEYC contributions:

> "We're Many Members, but One Body: Fostering a Healthy Self-Identity and Agency in African American Boys," in *Young Children* Vol. 70, No. 3 (2015)

> "Black Boys Matter: Cultivating Their Identity, Agency, and Voice," in *Teaching Young Children* Vol. 12, No. 3 (2019)

> "Black Boys Matter: Strategies for a Culturally Responsive Classroom," in *Teaching Young Children* Vol. 12, No. 4 (2019)

> *Each and Every Child: Teaching Preschool with an Equity Lens,* Chapters 12 and 13 (2020)

> "Tell Families, 'We See You and We Value Your Contribution,'" on the NAEYC Blog (2020)

> "Understanding the Sociocultural Context of Families is More Important Than Ever," on the NAEYC Blog (2020)

> "Supporting Teachers Through Change," in *Young Children* Vol. 75, No. 4 (2020)

> "Message in a Backpack™ Helping Your Child Through Change," in *Teaching Young Children* Vol. 14, No. 1 (2020)

> "Now Read This! Books that Promote Race, Identity, Agency, and Voice: Part 1," in *Teaching Young Children* Vol. 14, No. 1 (2020)

> *Advancing Equity and Embracing Diversity in Early Childhood Education: Elevating Voices and Actions,* Chapter 9 (2021)

> "Now Read This! Books that Promote Race, Identity, Agency, and Voice: Part 2," in *Teaching Young Children* Vol. 14, No. 2 (2021)

> *Developmentally Appropriate Practice in Early Childhood Programs Serving Children from Birth Through Age 8,* 4th ed, volume coeditor, Chapter 3 coauthor, Chapter 6 author (2022)

Reflection Questions

1. Think about the many dimensions of diversity (e.g., culture, language, gender identity, gender expression) in any group of children. In the children you teach or spend time with, what are those dimensions? To support your reflections, read the discussion of equity on pages 18–22 in *Developmentally Appropriate Practice* (NAEYC 2022).

2. "Creating a Caring, Equitable Community of Learners" is the first guideline of developmentally appropriate practice. What does *Developmentally Appropriate Practice* (NAEYC 2022), Chapter 6 especially, have to say about the importance of supporting children's voice and agency as part of this kind of community?

3. Consider times when children show that they notice cultural or racial differences. Build upon these observations to implement or role-play ways that you might use these times as essential opportunities to nurture all children's individuality and worth.

4. Choose an activity from this article and plan how you can implement it in your early learning setting. What challenges might you face and how could you address them?

5. Find several of the recommended authentic multicultural children's books, review them, and consider their potential value to the children and families in your early learning setting.

6. Think about the children you teach. Are there any you identify who especially need your support in cultivating and strengthening their voice and agency? As you work toward this goal, observe these children and document the effects of your efforts. See pages 20–22 in *Developmentally Appropriate Practice* (NAEYC 2022) for insights into children's individuality and contexts.

7. Reciprocal partnerships with families are essential to the work of giving all children voice and agency. Establishing respectful, reciprocal relationships is a starting point to building these reciprocal partnerships. For practices you might implement to develop these partnerships, review the detailed examples on pages 150–157 in *Developmentally Appropriate Practice* (NAEYC 2022).

Kendi, I.X. 2019. *How to Be an Antiracist.* New York: One World.

Kuh, L.P., D. LeeKeenan, H. Given, & M.R. Beneke. 2016. "Moving Beyond Anti-Bias Activities: Supporting the Development of Anti-Bias Practices." *Young Children* 71 (1): 58–65.

NAEYC. 2022. *Developmentally Appropriate Practice in Early Childhood Programs Serving Children from Birth Through Age 8.* 4th ed. Washington, DC: NAEYC.

OCR (US Department of Education Office of Civil Rights). 2014. *Data Snapshot: Early Childhood Education* (Issue Brief No. 2). Civil Rights Data Collection. www2.ed.gov/about/offices/list/ocr/docs/crdc-early-learning-snapshot.pdf.

Ramsey, P.G. 2015. *Teaching and Learning in a Diverse World: Multicultural Education for Young Children.* 4th ed. New York: Teachers College Press.

Souto-Manning, M. 2013. *Multicultural Teaching in the Early Childhood Classroom: Approaches, Strategies, and Tools Preschool–2nd Grade.* New York: Teachers College Press; Washington, DC: Association for Childhood Education International.

Wright, B.L. 2019. "Black Boys Matter: Cultivating Their Identity, Agency, and Voice." *Teaching Young Children* 12 (3): 4–7.

Wright, B.L., S.L. Counsell, & S.L. Tate. 2015. "We're Many Members, But One Body: Fostering a Healthy Self-Identity and Agency in African American Boys." *Young Children* 70 (3): 24–31.

Wright, B.L. With S.L. Counsell. 2018. *The Brilliance of Black Boys: Cultivating School Success in the Early Grades.* New York: Teachers College Press.

About the Author

Brian L. Wright, PhD, is associate professor and coordinator of the early childhood education program as well as coordinator of the middle school cohort of the African American Male Academy at the University of Memphis. He is author of *The Brilliance of Black Boys: Cultivating School Success in the Early Grades,* with contributions by Shelly L. Counsell, which won the National Association for Multicultural Education's 2018 Phillip C. Chinn Book Award.

Building Caring, Peaceful Communities

Just as "it takes a village to raise a child," the development of social and emotional competence and well-being requires a community. From NAEYC's 1996 position statement on developmentally appropriate practice to its most recent, creating a caring community of learners has been identified as one of six interrelated areas of practice. (The 2020 position statement saw the addition of *equitable* to this area of practice.) Group experiences can provide young children with a secure sense of belonging, affirming each child's identity within their social and cultural contexts. As children interact with one another in early childhood education settings, teachers intentionally guide them toward positive relationships and friendships, collaboration, and peaceful ways to handle inevitable conflicts. The fourth edition of *Developmentally Appropriate Practice* (NAEYC 2022) dedicates an entire chapter to this guideline and these related issues, emphasizing that learning communities are both caring and equitable and recommending specific strategies to nurture such communities at every age.

The three articles in this part help teachers create communities that welcome all children as valued members, supporting their emerging social skills and increasing their ability to care for one another.

In "Supporting Peer Relationships and Social Competence in Inclusive Preschool Programs," **Adam S. Kennedy** documents the importance of social skills development for all children. The author invites readers to promote each child's social development with experiences that respond to individual needs, abilities, and cultural and community contexts.

"Guidance Strategies to Prevent and Address Preschool Bullying" encourages teachers to use reciprocal, trusting relationships with children and families as the foundation of prevention and intervention. **Jill M. Raisor** and **Stacy D. Thompson** illustrate how teachers can model respect, kindness, and other prosocial behaviors as well as teach nonaggressive, assertive skills.

Veronica Benavides, Roxanne Ledda, and **Maimuna Mohammed** tell the story of how their classroom community engaged in social justice projects that increased children's empathy and sense of agency. "Never Too Young to Champion a Cause: Supporting Positive Identity Development Through Social Justice Curriculum in Preschool" may inspire your own collective action.

REFERENCE

NAEYC. 2022. *Developmentally Appropriate Practice in Early Childhood Programs Serving Children from Birth Through Age 8*. 4th ed. Washington, DC: NAEYC.

Supporting Peer Relationships and Social Competence in Inclusive Preschool Programs

Adam S. Kennedy

Ms. Renee is supporting three children in a block-building activity, playing alongside them and offering narration, reinforcement, and thoughtful questions. Jacob, a 3½-year-old child with autism spectrum disorder, runs excitedly into the block center, kicking the blocks in all directions. Latrice yells, "Jacob, you're stupid!"

Maya is a younger preschooler in Ms. Leo's classroom, with large and small motor limitations related to cerebral palsy. Four-year-old Destiny notices Maya making rainbows on the wall with a prism from the small motor center. "Lemme see!" Destiny exclaims, grabbing the prism from Maya's hand. Destiny fails to recognize this opportunity to explore a shared interest with her classmate.

xamples such as these illustrate typical conflicts that may occur in preschool classrooms. Like conflicts among all young children, those involving young children with disabilities or other unique learning needs serve as windows into children's social and emotional skills and needs. They also highlight teaching opportunities. Teachers play an essential role in showing preschoolers how to manage peer relationships successfully. Peer conflict is typical for young children but still requires teacher assessment. Paying special attention to children's interactions in inclusive classrooms can allow teachers to take full advantage of opportunities to maximize the meaningful participation of children with disabilities and encourage early friendships to blossom among all the children.

Teachers in inclusive classrooms strive to provide individualized education to young children with disabilities alongside their peers. For all children to learn and develop successfully, it is important for general and special education teachers to engage in extensive and meaningful collaboration with each other, families, and all service providers who work with a child to target areas of need—including speech-language pathologists, occupational therapists, and nurses. One of the primary goals of inclusive programs is to create an atmosphere in which positive peer relationships can flourish. In such programs, children with disabilities have full access to all aspects of the learning environment, opportunities to participate actively, and adequate supports for success (DEC & NAEYC 2009).

Social Skills and the Importance of Peer Relationships for Young Children

Social skills and social competence are key areas of preschool teaching and learning. In the preschool years, most children learn to successfully navigate a complex world of friendships and adult relationships in environments with new rules, routines, and expectations for behaviors like waiting, conversing, sharing small and large group spaces, and taking turns. Peer-related *social competence* can be thought of as the overall success of preschoolers in achieving social goals, interacting with others, and fitting in with their peers. Teachers of young children help all children to increase their competence—often by working on social skills during classroom activities and routines. *Social skills* include all of the behaviors children use with others as they gain social competence, including cooperating, initiating conversations, and handling conflicts by managing their emotions and engaging in joint problem solving.

Children experience many new opportunities in preschool to use social skills and understand them with greater depth. They develop some of their first friendships, learn to follow a few classroom rules and routines, and develop ever stronger emotional control. Intentional teaching and teacher-supported peer interactions enhance children's abilities to use social language and read other children's social cues. These abilities help children increase the success of their social initiations and responses. Basic social skills both predict and pave the way for more complex ones (such as sharing, negotiating play roles, and dealing with conflict) and support learning-related social skills (such as remaining on task and organizing materials for classwork).

Successful interactions with peers provide both opportunities for and a pathway to social and emotional development and continued learning in kindergarten and beyond. For example, when a skilled teacher is present to provide support, children can learn and practice skills such as perspective taking, empathy,

Teachers Create Supportive Environments When They . . .

> Design learning centers that create small group social environments

> Are socially competent play partners, modeling what play conversations sound like

> Model play that includes children with disabilities

> Provide open-ended materials (blocks, clothing for dramatic play, natural materials) that stimulate conversation

> Encourage children to engage with each other and ask questions

> Keep a strong presence during center time, offering problem-solving assistance as necessary

> Assist with children's diverse ways of initiating play with one another

> Incorporate activities that allow children in inclusive classrooms to get to know each other, such as circle time songs and activities that emphasize friendship, children's names, and their similarities and differences

and extending conversation through group games and social play. These benefits also reinforce cognitive development, as developmentally younger children reap the benefits of playing with classmates who have more advanced skills.

Preschool provides key opportunities to set in place the framework on which all of these sophisticated skills are built. Teachers in inclusive classrooms can strengthen this foundation by bringing social play and activities to the forefront during classroom planning. They accomplish this by making sure the classroom allows for as many social opportunities as possible and that teachers are actively involved in helping children make sense and take advantage of these opportunities. While all classrooms are inherently social communities, inclusive classrooms require teachers to think beyond creating an environment where communication can simply *happen*. Teachers play a critical role in helping children understand how social interactions begin and end and how to sustain them in ways that the children find meaningful and enjoyable.

Social Competence in Young Children with Disabilities and Other Challenges

In inclusive classrooms with children who function at varied developmental levels and who have unique needs, teachers can observe the impact of disabilities and risk factors (such as social isolation or limited prior experience interacting with peers) on children's social interactions. For example, conflict may arise when a child enters play disruptively because she has not yet learned other ways to join in. Alternatively, children with motor delays might miss out on opportunities to engage in group play because they need additional time to move from place to place. Any disability (including autism spectrum disorder, developmental delays, and visual or hearing impairments) can have an impact on a young child's play and early friendships, so understanding each child's strengths and needs is essential.

Recognizing strengths and needs. Do not assume that all children with a particular disability will look and behave in the same ways. For example, a developmental delay might affect a child's frequency of play with peers, his physical ability to join rough-and-tumble play, or the ways in which he reacts to frustration in play. For another child with a developmental delay, however, peer relationships might actually be an area of strength. All children hold the potential to learn social skills, experience friendship, and grow in their social competence. Supportive social environments set the stage for strengths-based teaching and learning; the next step is to observe and collect information about the social interactions of all the children in the group.

Encouraging social interactions. A clear picture of the social world of the classroom allows teachers to identify social situations in which children with disabilities or other needs might need support to navigate successfully. One of these situations is social rejection, which has been consistently noted in research on preschoolers in inclusive programs (e.g., Bulotsky-Shearer et al. 2010; Odom et al. 2006). Young children with disabilities tend to play with others less frequently and have fewer conversations than their peers who do not have disabilities; they may also lose social skills more quickly if the skills they do have are not used consistently and successfully, reinforced by teachers, or acknowledged by peers. This means that children with disabilities might have fewer natural opportunities to develop their social skills. Inclusive educators can open the door to early friendships that not only transcend disabilities but also endure beyond preschool by proactively addressing social readiness.

For example, Nimona is a 3-year-old with cognitive, motor, and communication delays associated with Down syndrome. In comparison to other children, Nimona needs significantly more peer interactions to learn an important skill (such as imitating and expanding on a peer's play). If she has only half the opportunities because she is frequently in situations where she is isolated or rejected, then her social development may hit a roadblock. This scenario illustrates one example of why children with disabilities may have fewer friendships than their peers. You can minimize roadblocks such as these by focusing attention on children's interests, strengths, and typical interaction patterns. Then use this information to select themes, materials, and activities that are accessible to every child. Knowing a lot about Nimona's disability provides little guidance; however, knowing that she likes to talk about dogs and spends most of her free time at the art center allows for thoughtful planning of interactive experiences in which you can positively guide play and conversation.

Reviewing IEPs. The answers to some questions may be found in a child's Individualized Education Program (IEP). From the age of 3 on, every child with a disability must have an IEP, developed by a multidisciplinary team of professionals (including the teacher and caregivers) with input from the child's family. The IEP outlines the child's current functioning across all developmental domains as well as her needs and strengths. The IEP also lays out individualized goals and strategies for achieving those goals (IDEA 2004). However, while a child's IEP should identify any needed goals for development of social skills, young children may achieve those goals more quickly than anticipated. Furthermore, an IEP cannot always take into account all of the varied opportunities for a preschooler to work on social skills throughout the program day. Careful observation must focus on the here and now to identify areas of strength and difficulty and document children's progress toward achieving their goals. Peer relationships provide perhaps the best indicator of this progress (Odom et al. 2006).

Use Observation to Determine . . .

> Each child's current social skills

> Areas of strength and growth for all children

> Children's individual interests

> Times when each child is most likely to interact with peers

> The level of inclusion for each child during play

> Each child's ability to initiate interactions and to respond to the initiations of others

> Where and when conflicts occur most frequently

> Whether any child is being socially rejected

Like every other aspect of children's development, social skills develop at varying rates and in unique ways; as teachers do for every other area of development, they must individualize their expectations for young children's social behavior. While educators are generally prepared to assess, address, and intervene to support children's developmental needs, developmentally appropriate practice (DAP) to support social competence involves a dynamic relationship between school and family that requires shared understandings of the complex nature of children's behavior in school.

DAP includes shaping the environment of the classroom (including rules and expectations for children's behavior) based, in part, upon the values, expectations, and behavioral and linguistic conventions children experience in their homes and communities. Educators must treat these conventions as more than pieces of information to collect. They should be the themes of communication and relationship building with families.

This article contains examples of child behaviors that are complex, challenging, and/or easily misunderstood. When attempting to understand a behavior that appears to be maladaptive or hurtful, work with your colleagues to evaluate not just the child but also the social context of the child's behavior. Collaboratively observing both the learning environment and teacher instruction can help to identify some of the ways in which these may contribute to or prevent behaviors that interfere with children's social success. This collaboration must include families in order for educational decisions and practices to respect, integrate, and sustain family beliefs and practices around social interaction.

Intentional planning will help you successfully support preschoolers' social competence and social communication. Employ your expertise and that of your team members to effectively plan for and implement interventions with children. Discuss with families some of the many naturalistic ways in which social skills are a part of the daily routine, and work directly with them to support them in their interaction skills. Remember that each young child (including those with disabilities and other unique learning needs) is a member of a family and community, and you will have greater success in your work when you acknowledge and seek to better understand children's contexts outside of school. This requires humility, reflection, a desire to express empathy, an awareness of your own beliefs about what is socially appropriate, and skills in relationship building. If you embark on deepening these skills and understandings, you'll be well equipped for helping young children navigate their social world.

Seeking explanations. When observing and assessing young children, it is helpful to look beyond social behaviors and seek explanations for what you see. Two children might use the same behavior—for example, failing to respond to other children's play invitations—for very different reasons. For example, Ms. Renee observes that Kenny takes several minutes to respond when Foster asks to share his blocks. Rather than stopping the observation to insist that Kenny share, Ms. Renee continues to observe so she can collect more information. Later, she will review the observation notes from this incident and others, and discuss with her coteacher possible explanations for what she saw. They might ask, *Does Kenny seem to understand what Foster is asking? Does he need extra time to respond? Is paired block building with a peer new to him?* Answers to these questions help Ms. Renee plan appropriate ways to support the children's play and determine which social skills to focus on for each.

If the issue is related to Kenny's ability to understand or become familiar with the social experience, Ms. Renee might engage Kenny in play, incorporating the vocabulary and behaviors associated with cooperative center play. If Kenny needs additional time to respond, then Ms. Renee might work with Foster on waiting a sufficient length of time after asking Kenny a question. This may allow both children to succeed, and it serves to decrease their frustration. The table titled "Addressing Social Competence Concerns" on pages 40–41 provides additional examples of behaviors that sometimes cause concern about children's social competence, possible explanations for these behaviors, things to keep in mind when assessing the situation, and teaching strategies to increase social competence.

Promoting Social Competence in Inclusive Classrooms

Children who lack the social skills to interact successfully with their peers are likely to need specific opportunities to learn those skills. Inclusive classrooms present a unique opportunity for children with disabilities to build these skills with consistent, competent peer models. But how should teachers intervene? What should the interventions look like?

Evidence-based preschool social competence interventions often involve teacher-led social skills activities followed by positive guidance during play. In other words, using a variety of strategies, teachers help children learn and master the skills, including offering support during the times when children have natural opportunities to use them. In some cases, teachers may directly teach social behaviors (such as greetings or requests for toys) and then follow up with guidance during play. For example, at circle time Ms. Leon and the children sing a new song about inviting others to play. She then follows the children to the learning centers, watches and listens as some children try this new behavior, and supports children who are playing alone or who seem ready to learn to invite a friend to join them. Some children might respond to a prompt; others might need Ms. Leon to model what to say and do: "Hannah, when you finish your puzzle would you like to play a game with me?"

Strategies for teaching children social skills can include direct lessons, songs, group activities, or simply joint play. Ms. Lynne, for instance, models skills such as requesting, questioning, commenting, and sharing while partnering with children in pretend play in the dramatic play area. She takes advantage of these natural opportunities, acknowledging children when they use these behaviors ("Marlee is sharing the pans with Tina very nicely"), and helping children with disabilities to respond positively ("Anthony would like to eat with us. How can we find out what he would like to eat?"). Everyday routines such as meals and snack times also provide natural opportunities to address social skills. Children can practice social skills such as greeting, turn taking, questioning and responding, requesting, and saying thank you. In inclusive classrooms, teachers emphasize as many of these natural opportunities as possible, supplementing them with more explicit lessons or activities when needed (Sainato et al. 2008). The table titled "Addressing Social Competence Concerns" on pages 40–41 provides several more examples of these activities as they relate to specific concerns teachers might have regarding young children with disabilities.

Addressing Social Competence Concerns

Social Competence Concern	Some Possible Explanations
Tari (age 4) tends to enter play disruptively, often bumping into other children and knocking over their toys.	› Tari might not understand what's expected when asking to join in other children's play. › She might need a high level of sensory stimulation in play to maintain her alertness and interest.
Marcus (age 3½) hesitates or fails to respond to most play invitations, although he appears interested.	› Marcus might not understand or recognize these as invitations to play. › He might not hear what other children are saying. › He might need additional time to respond. › He might be a child who is typically shy or slow to join in.
Naomi (age 4½) prefers solo, parallel play over cooperative play. She spends the majority of her choice time painting or molding with clay.	› Naomi might be shy or anxious around peers. › She may simply prefer solitary play. › Some children may need an adult to bridge the gap between parallel and cooperative play and spark their interest in social activity.
Leo and Carmen (4-year-olds who do not have disabilities) share the large motor play space with their classmates but seem to engage in few conversations with the children in the class who have language delays or impairments.	› Children with language delays/impairments are likely to converse less. › Some children are unfamiliar with play-related conversation.
JC (age 5) tends to follow his friends in play, rather than taking on the role of leader.	› Children who are developmentally advanced often make a strong impression as leaders and models for less advanced peers. The less advanced peer might not be motivated to or see a way to take the lead. › How much is known about JC's interests and play behaviors outside of school? › Is JC comfortable and familiar with the classroom?

Things to Keep in Mind When Assessing the Situation	Teaching Strategies to Increase Social Competence
> Behaviors such as these are not always signs of aggression. Sometimes they indicate that a child is not aware of the feelings and perspectives of other children. Is Tari at a developmental stage where she should be aware of the feelings and perspectives of others?	> Write and illustrate a Social Story™ to help Tari learn the steps, language, and feelings that may be involved in choosing and approaching other children to play with in a learning center. > Schedule a planning time when children state their play ideas and choose partners before moving to learning centers.
> Try to observe Marcus in several situations with different play partners. > Difficulties with hearing, understanding, and responding each require a different strategy.	> Model how to respond when invited to play; make sure to provide Marcus with other opportunities to play with his classmates throughout the day (such as supporting his conversations and interactions with playmates during mealtimes and exploration of centers). > Consider the kind of language preschoolers must be able to use and understand in order to invite potential playmates and respond to their invitations.
> Avoid jumping to conclusions. Solo play is developmentally appropriate for preschoolers. It can be purposeful, exploratory, and creative—in other words, not a concern at all. Concerns arise when play seems anxious, repetitive, or purposeless. For example, a child who shows consistent interest in art materials should raise no concern; however, if a child simply bangs markers on the table without ever exploring their possibilities, then a closer look is warranted.	> Practice communication skills with children. Do not assume they know how to initiate and sustain conversation on a shared topic. > Use parallel play with Naomi's preferred toys as a starting point for engaging her.
> Play opportunities should encourage ongoing conversation. It can help to offer open-ended materials and sufficient time in areas such as the sand table and blocks. These will encourage a variety of types of exploratory play that may be observed, assessed, and supported.	> Encourage peers across the spectrum of social competence to play together. > Join children as a play partner; model the kinds of phrases and questions children can use during a conversation. Respond to and expand on children's comments and questions. > Ensure that the language needs of all children are addressed and that dual language learners are provided enough support. For example, label materials with multiple languages and images and help children communicate with one another during play.
> Not every child is a leader in play, and few children lead all of the time. Support children's growing competence, comfort, and problem solving in play situations by acknowledging their emerging competence and building their self-esteem. This still does not necessarily mean that every child has to take charge.	> Offer a descriptive commentary that acknowledges when children do take a leadership role. > Offer games and activities in response to a child's interests so that he feels more comfortable and competent taking a leadership role in play.

The Big Picture: Social Competence and Young Children's Worlds

Efforts to teach social skills and increase social competence may be more successful when teachers know how they relate to each child's overall social and emotional development. Young children's relationships extend far beyond the walls of the classroom, so it is essential to consider not only play-related social skills but also cognitive and language capabilities and individual personalities.

Cultural factors play an enormous role in social development. They may also explain many of the differences in children's styles of interactions. Consider what social behaviors are valued and encouraged in each child's family and community. What skills does the child need to succeed at home? On the playground? With playmates outside of school? Teachers must maintain an openness to learning about each child's culture, key relationships, and life outside the classroom through collaboration with family members. These collaborations broaden the view of children's strengths to include the unique assets of families and communities.

Families can be successfully included in social competence interventions. Keep them informed about work on social competence in the classroom and solicit their input, finding out how they address social skills at home. Consistency between home and school routines can be especially beneficial for children who have difficulty navigating such routines. Collaborating with families also represents an essential component of addressing the needs of culturally and linguistically diverse young children with disabilities. Teachers use what they learn to better understand the meaning of children's social behavior not only in the classroom but in light of each family's perspectives, communication preferences, and interaction style (Derman-Sparks & Edwards with Goins 2020). This understanding, in turn, enhances the responsiveness of their teaching to each family's and child's needs.

Conclusion

To succeed in kindergarten, children need not only basic academic skills but also well-developed social skills (Missall & Hojnoski 2008). Addressing the social competence and interaction skills of young children is an ongoing process that involves continuous planning, teaching, assessment, and reflection throughout the year. Implementing more targeted strategies might take a few days to a few weeks, but creating a positive inclusive environment requires teachers to establish a foundation and then collaborate, plan, teach, observe, and reflect consistently throughout the year. Keep in mind that success in one area is not the end of the story! For instance, when a teacher is successful in getting children to initiate play more often, play initiations will increase but so might conflict. Problem solving then becomes the next focus of social skill learning. When these processes are in place, teachers are much more likely to create warm, nurturing, inclusive environments that lead to meaningful, long-lasting social and academic benefits for young children.

REFERENCES

Bulotsky-Shearer, R.J., X. Domínguez, E.R. Bell, H.L. Rouse, & J.W. Fantuzzo. 2010. "Relations Between Behavior Problems in Classroom Social and Learning Situations and Peer Social Competence in Head Start and Kindergarten." *Journal of Emotional and Behavioral Disorders* (18) 4: 195–210.

DEC (Division for Early Childhood) & NAEYC. 2009. "Early Childhood Inclusion." Joint position statement. Chapel Hill: The University of North Carolina, FPG Child Development Institute. www.naeyc.org/files/naeyc/file/positions/DEC_NAEYC_EC_updatedKS.pdf.

Derman-Sparks, L., & J.O. Edwards. With C.M. Goins. 2020. *Anti-Bias Education for Young Children and Ourselves.* 2nd ed. Washington, DC: NAEYC.

IDEA (Individuals with Disabilities Education Act). 2004. 20 U.S.C. § 1400.

Missall, K.N., & R.L. Hojnoski. 2008. "The Critical Nature of Young Children's Emerging Peer-Related Social Competence for Transition to School." Chap. 6 in *Social Competence of Young Children: Risk, Disability, and Intervention,* eds. W.H. Brown, S.L. Odom, & S.R. McConnell, 117–37. Baltimore: Brookes.

NAEYC. 2022. *Developmentally Appropriate Practice in Early Childhood Programs Serving Children from Birth Through Age 8.* 4th ed. Washington, DC: NAEYC.

Odom, S., C. Zercher, S. Li, J. Marquart, S. Sandall, & W. Brown. 2006. "Social Acceptance and Rejection of Children with Disabilities: A Mixed-Method Analysis." *Journal of Educational Psychology* 98 (4): 807–23.

Sainato, D., S. Jung, M. Salmon, & J. Axe. 2008. "Classroom Influences on Young Children's Emerging Social Competence." Chap. 5 in *Social Competence of Young Children: Risk, Disability, and Intervention,* eds. W.H. Brown, S.L. Odom, & S.R. McConnell, 99–116. Baltimore: Brookes.

About the Author

Adam S. Kennedy, PhD, is associate professor of early childhood special education (ECSE) at Loyola University Chicago. Adam coordinates a field-based teacher education program that blends early childhood education and ECSE. He conducts research on field-based teacher education, inclusive practices, and LGBT+ social justice in early childhood education. He is also the author of the *Early Pride Matters* website.

Reflection Questions

1. Describe preschoolers you believe to be socially competent. What do you see in their interactions and behavior? What might these perceptions say about your beliefs or biases regarding child development?

2. Think about two children with whom you work or know well who differ from each other in some aspects of social and cultural contexts (e.g., ability, language, ethnicity). In your early learning program, do you sometimes notice others showing different expectations for these children's social competence based on these differences?

3. According to this article, is it appropriate to have different expectations for different children? Do you agree, and why? Share examples from your personal or professional experience.

4. The importance of peer relationships is addressed throughout *Developmentally Appropriate Practice* (NAEYC 2022), including in relation to play and problem solving, small group learning with peers, and children's observations of how they are similar to and different from their peers. From the perspective of developmentally appropriate practice, why is it important to support children's peer relationships from the toddler years onward? Based on your experience and this article, what strategies may be helpful?

5. Think about a child you know who has a disability. Describe this child's strengths, and consider how you could build on those strengths to enhance the child's peer relationships and overall social competence.

6. How might you collaborate with families who may be facing a variety of challenges to better understand and support their children's social and emotional development? Plan specific strategies to strengthen such collaboration. For guidance on engaging in reciprocal family partnerships, see the examples discussed across pages 150–157 in *Developmentally Appropriate Practice* (NAEYC 2022).

Guidance Strategies to Prevent and Address Preschool Bullying

Jill M. Raisor and Stacy D. Thompson

In the children's book *The Recess Queen,* by Alexis O'Neill, illustrated by Laura Huliska-Beith, "Mean Jean" dominates the playground. The children are intimidated by her until Katie Sue, a new child, arrives. Katie Sue courageously asks Mean Jean why she is so bossy, and then offers to jump rope with her. No one has ever dared invite Mean Jean to play, so everyone watches in shock to see the reaction from the stunned Mean Jean. On the next page, Mean Jean and Katie Sue giggle and jump rope together. From that day on, Mean Jean does not have time to bully the children because she is too busy playing with her new friends.

In the media, bullying is cited as one of the challenges many children face. It is not as apparent from media reports that bullying behaviors can begin at an early age (Macintyre 2009); however, with early intervention some bullying behaviors can be reduced or possibly even prevented. This article presents an approach involving children, educators, and families working together to address aggressive behavior among young children that can lead to bullying.

As educators, we strive to be intentional in modeling best practices for children and families when addressing serious issues such as bullying. Teachers establishing reciprocal relationships with families is integral to the development of the whole child (NAEYC 2022). Strategies such as developing positive relationships with families, along with a planned approach of prevention and intervention, can build children's self-regulation skills and empower bystanders to act when witnessing bullying behavior—ultimately resulting in decreased bullying (Ahmed 2008; Gartrell & Gartrell 2008).

Bullying behavior is not acceptable at any age. An aggressive behavior can evolve into bullying when it is a negative action implemented and repeated over time (Olweus 2003). It is best to step in to address these situations early and follow up with continuous reminders and positive guidance so children can learn appropriate ways to express feelings and desires. As a starting point, open the lines of communication with children by discussing bullying. An effective way to begin this conversation is by reading books together and discussing them. Lacina and Stetson (2013) list multiple resources and strategies for using literature in this manner with children in the primary grades. Preschool teachers can adapt the suggestions to engage children in a picture walk—a strategy using a book's illustrations to discuss the meaning of the text—or have conversations about the characters and actions in a book to encourage sharing ideas.

Bullying Defined

According to Olweus (2003), being bullied means "being exposed, repeatedly and over time, to negative actions on the part of one or more other students" (12). In addition, Olweus (2003) states that there is an imbalance of power (e.g., a stronger child pushing a smaller child). Children as young as 3 begin to form social hierarchies (Macintyre 2009). Some children may be more popular among their classmates than others who tend to take a less assertive role. By age 4, bullying behavior may emerge (Macintyre 2009) whereby certain children intentionally exclude others from play or target them for teasing.

One of the first steps should be to discuss and define aggressive behavior that can lead to bullying and what this looks like to children. An example of bullying would be a group of girls deliberately excluding another girl from play, telling her repeatedly that she's not allowed to join them. When reading aloud stories, discuss with children how the characters respond to the bullying situation and whether their responses are effective. This encourages children to share their own experiences with the adult, allows them the opportunity to ask questions, and reassures them that the teacher is concerned about their well-being. We recommend adapting children's books that address bullying, such as *Chrysanthemum*, by Kevin Henkes (kindergarten–grade 2), to make them appropriate for preschoolers. (See "Children's Books About Aggression and Bullying Behavior" on page 48 for a summary of the children's books mentioned in this article.)

Families play an important role in children's social and emotional development. For young children learning to process social situations, having a safe setting in which to share, brainstorm, and role-play a social situation they encountered at school can help build resiliency and assertiveness. A game in which family members share the high (best) and low (worst) parts of their day can offer a beneficial start to meaningful conversations and fostering children's relational skills. This game allows an equal opportunity for everyone to contribute.

Consider sharing this game with families to participate in at home. Here is an example of how they might introduce the game:

Adult: I had an interesting day. Remember that piece of jewelry I showed you that I've been working on all week? Today I finally finished it! That was the best part of my day. It's been exciting to work on a design I haven't done before, and I can't wait to share it with the client who ordered it! Let's go around the table and all share the best part of our day. I am interested to learn more about your day.

Each member shares something if she chooses to. Acknowledge each contribution.

Adult: I also had a low part to my day when I missed an important phone call from someone. I tried to return their call, but they didn't answer. I hope I don't miss an opportunity to sell something to them. Did you have a low part to your day? What didn't go like you hoped it would?

Each member shares if he chooses to. Thank the sharers for talking about part of their day, and process possible solutions together if appropriate. If someone chooses to not share, remind him that he is welcome to do so later.

Encourage families to actively listen to each person as events are discussed. Each member could brainstorm possible reasons for the behavior of the person(s) involved in an interaction. This helps the child learn to take different perspectives and encourages her not to personalize another person's behavior. Next, family members might discuss different ways the child could have responded. This may assist the child in addressing and/or coping with unpleasant or unforeseen situations and problem solve for the future. Other children in the family often provide original perspectives and ideas to support their siblings.

A relaxed setting encourages everyone to feel comfortable sharing. For some families, this might be dinnertime or bedtime; for others, the daily ride home from school offers an opportunity to share their experiences. This game also acknowledges the important contribution each person makes to the family. If the game is played consistently, children may be encouraged to view this as a regular opportunity to talk about their day.

Bullying in Preschool

Young children may learn behaviors such as name calling from interactions with adult family members or older siblings, or from exposure to inappropriate television shows, videos, or movies. Such behaviors, when not addressed, can lead to bullying. Therefore, early childhood is an optimal time for knowledgeable, caring adults to implement prosocial strategies that identify and reduce these behaviors. The preschool years in particular are a critical time for guiding young children's social development. Preschool is often the first time children are learning to collaborate with others in a peer group.

Piaget and Inhelder (1967) believed preschoolers seek out understanding of their environments through negotiations with others over objects. These interactions provide information for them to construct an understanding of their peers. For example, Rory wants to play with a puzzle that Meiling has just taken off the puzzle rack. Rory must learn to wait his turn or approach Meiling to see if she wants to work on the puzzle together. In preschool settings, young children can learn how to practice these social skills with adult guidance and supervision.

Three Types of Aggression in the Preschool Years

For preschoolers, a combination of developmental and environmental factors may play a role in using aggressive behaviors that over time could become bullying. Three distinct types of aggression frequently occur in the preschool years: physical, instrumental, and relational.

Physical Aggression

> Katya, a 5-year-old, is frequently physically aggressive toward Sera. When Katya notices that her teacher is distracted, she kicks Sera.

Socialization skills are just emerging in preschool, so many children are not familiar with sharing toys, space, and the teacher's time with other children. This sometimes results in physically aggressive behavior, such as hitting, pinching, pushing, and kicking. When there is an imbalance of power between children, it can lead to bullying to achieve dominance. *The Grouchy Ladybug,* by Eric Carle (preschool–grade 2), addresses physical aggression.

Children's Books About Aggression and Bullying Behavior

A Bad Case of Stripes
By David Shannon (1998)

Preschool–Grade 2. Camilla Cream loves lima beans, but she will not eat them because other children at her school do not like them and she wants to fit in. She goes through a series of strange physical transformations, such as waking up with stripes on her body. These continue until she is forced to eat her lima beans. Through these experiences, she discovers that being a unique individual is perfectly acceptable.

Chrysanthemum
By Kevin Henkes (1991)

Kindergarten–Grade 2. Chrysanthemum likes her name until she begins school and her classmates tease her. Her spirit is restored when she learns that her beloved music teacher, Mrs. Twinkle, has a unique name herself and is considering naming her baby Chrysanthemum.

The Grouchy Ladybug
By Eric Carle (1996)

Preschool–Grade 2. The Grouchy Ladybug is always ready to fight any creature that crosses his path. He displays a lot of aggression, until the day he meets a blue whale, who helps him become better behaved.

Stand Tall, Molly Lou Melon
By Patty Lovell, illustrated by David Catrow (2001)

Preschool–Grade 2. Molly Lou Melon relies on advice from her grandma as she begins school and is confronted by an aggressive peer. Her spirited personality and positive self-esteem shine as she is able to put a positive spin on the social situation.

When Sophie Gets Angry—Really, Really Angry . . .
By Molly Bang (1999)

Preschool–Grade 2. Sophie is playing with her toy, but her sister wants it and Sophie has to give it to her. This makes Sophie angry—really, really angry. Then, to make matters worse, she trips over a toy. Sophie ultimately learns how to cope with her intense angry feelings with help from an adult.

Instrumental Aggression

Three-year-old Sayf insists that he is the only one who can play with the green ball. When any other child tries to play with it, Sayf grabs the ball and sometimes pushes the other child away.

In young preschoolers, behaviors such as hitting, pushing, and grabbing to get a desired toy or snack are common. This object-oriented aggression is called *instrumental aggression.* Its emergence could be due in part to a combination of developmental and environmental factors. At this age, many children are unable to understand or take the perspective of another (Piaget & Inhelder 1967). Also, some preschool-age children (particularly young ones) lack the language skills and ability to accurately express their wants and needs. Over time, instrumental aggression can evolve into bullying when it is repeated and there is an imbalance of power between the children. Share Molly Bang's *When Sophie Gets Angry— Really, Really Angry . . .* (preschool–grade 2) with your class.

Relational Aggression

Elizabeth, who is 4, wants to join a small group of girls playing. She asks, "Can I play with you?" Romana, speaking for the group, responds, "Yes, but only if you are the little sister and do not talk." Thus, the acceptance is conditional.

Teachers and families may hear 4- and 5-year-olds engaged in exclusionary interactions such as "You can't come to my birthday party!" or "I won't be your friend." When these behaviors are repeated and elevated to hurtful levels, they are called *relational aggression,* which is "the intent to harm others by removing or threatening to damage a relationship or feelings of social acceptance and inclusion in social groups" (Ostrov et al. 2004, 356). Frequent and extreme use of relational aggression is a form of bullying. Trying hard to fit in is the topic of *A Bad Case of Stripes,* by David Shannon (preschool–grade 2).

Social Processing

According to Dodge and Crick (1990), children go through five steps when processing information about their social world. The first step is *decoding social cues.* For example, when a child drinking from a water fountain is pushed from behind, she immediately looks around to see what is happening. Next, she *interprets.* That is, she hears children laughing (though their laughter may be unrelated) and thinks someone pushed her on purpose or that the children are laughing because they think the pushing is funny. The third and fourth steps involve *considering and evaluating an optimal response.* Depending on her interpretation of the event, she might consider taking physical action against another child, telling a teacher, ignoring the action, or stating that she does not like being pushed. Finally, she *enacts the response.* The child decides which is the best response and takes action. The decision is somewhat based on her knowledge of social interactions and a social-cognitive understanding of the consequences.

Strategies for Helping Children Who Use Bullying Behaviors

If children's use of aggression reaches a severe level, it is vital for teachers and other adults to address the behavior and help children learn how to use acceptable, positive behaviors. If these types of behaviors are not addressed during early childhood, they are likely to continue and could result in antisocial behaviors (NAEYC 2022). Young children actively write internal scripts for how to behave and react in social situations. Therefore, it is up to teachers and families to model and promote perspective taking. One strategy is role-playing, so children who struggle with reading emotional cues can observe multiple

For Further Reading

> **The Center on the Social and Emotional Foundations for Early Learning** (http://csefel.vanderbilt.edu) focuses on promoting the social and emotional development and school readiness of children from birth through age 5. The website offers resources in English and Spanish for families, trainers, teachers, caregivers, and administrators.

> ***Class Meetings: Young Children Solving Problems Together,* Rev. Ed**, by Emily Vance (NAEYC, 2014), highlights class meetings as opportunities for teachers to guide children in prosocial behaviors such as problem solving and conflict resolution.

> The **Conscious Discipline** program (http://consciousdiscipline.com), developed by Becky Bailey, is a comprehensive program that integrates social and emotional learning and behavior guidance. Conscious Discipline for Educators empowers adults to consciously respond to conflict, transforming it into an opportunity to teach young children critical life skills.

> The **Devereux Center for Resilient Children** (www.centerforresilientchildren.org) has a mission "to promote social and emotional development, foster resilience, and build skills for school and life success in children birth through school-age, as well as to promote the resilience of the adults who care for them." This site offers tips, strategies, and activities as well as additional web links to resources.

> ***The New Bully Free Classroom: Proven Prevention and Intervention Strategies for Teachers K–8***, by Allen L. Beane (Free Spirit, 2011), includes tips and strategies for teachers to help school-age children identify bullying and empower bystanders to take action. Some of the strategies can be adapted for early childhood settings and situations.

> **"Using Children's Literature to Support Positive Behaviors,"** by Jan Lacina and Ranae Stetson (*Young Children,* November 2013), recommends children's literature for helping children cope with difficult situations. Additionally, it details strategies for discussing the books with children.

responses to a situation and practice perspective taking. Together, teachers and children can discuss and determine which is the best choice. This activity easily lends itself to other integrated teaching strategies, such as making prediction charts and journaling.

Prediction charts allow children to document informed guesses about what might happen next. The teacher discusses the possible scenarios with the children and the class comes to a consensus about which prediction makes the most sense. Journaling encourages children to write or draw from various perspectives. For example, after hearing *The Three Little Pigs*, a child might first journal from the pigs' viewpoint and then from the big, bad wolf's.

Strategies for Children

It is important to encourage children to practice how they will respond and react to bullying behavior so they feel prepared the next time they experience it. Freedman (1999) suggests that teachers encourage children to use the following strategies, which can be adapted for preschoolers, to empower children and reduce their feelings of helplessness.

> Ignore the teasing only when it is appropriate and helpful to do so (in prolonged situations, other strategies are needed).

> Use I-messages to communicate ("It hurts my feelings when you tease me. Please stop").

> Agree with the facts (a girl teases a boy about his new glasses, and the boy agrees, "Yes, I do have new glasses").

> Ask a question about the behavior ("Why are you teasing me about my glasses?").

> Use positive self-talk (a boy tells himself, "I like my new glasses").

> Reframe; change a negative statement into a compliment ("Thank you, my glasses are new").

> Ask for help.

Depending on the individual child's situation, the effectiveness of these strategies varies. If the bullying persists, seek out additional suggestions and resources for administrators, teachers, and families at the Olweus Bullying Prevention Program website, Violence Prevention Works! (www .violencepreventionworks.org/public/bullying.page). Another resource is available at www.stopbullying.gov.

The most important concept for all children to learn is that bullying behavior is not acceptable and will not be allowed. Ensuring that all classmates, families, and staff take a firm stand against bullying and report bullying behavior sends a clear message that bullying behavior has consequences. Establish classroom rules about bullying and hold class meetings to discuss appropriate responses to bullying situations.

Gartrell and Gartrell (2008) recommend creating an "encouraging classroom" that emphasizes empathy and working with others to develop trust among students. For example, in Paley's (1992) seminal *You Can't Say You Can't Play,* she says children have the right to choose their friends but must be kind to everyone. Another option is to implement an anti-bullying curriculum. A good curriculum plan would include consultants who provide easily implemented strategies that resonate with personal values, as well as parents, teachers, and others who have relationships with the children.

Everyone involved (e.g., families, bystanders, child who is being bullied, and aggressor) must be on board and supportive of a bullying-free environment. This type of environment ensures that children have a mutual respect for others. This is critical for success. Identify areas where aggression and possible bullying behaviors are likely to occur, such as the playground, dramatic play area, and the block area. It is important to increase supervision in these areas. In addition, teachers can be sure to engage and interact with children to support their play and learning.

Families can get involved by sharing with teachers the concerns that children express at home about their peers. Encouraging a sense that "this is a safe place and bullying is not acceptable" should help prevent behaviors that may lead to bullying.

Strategies for Supporting Children Who Are Bullied

Children who are bullied also need assistance from caring adults. Being bullied can have long-term psychological effects such as low self-esteem and negative self-concept. Macintyre (2009) states that among other things, children with low self-esteem may become afraid to try new things, be easily frustrated, use aggression, and even start bullying others.

We, as educators, can create a safe environment to reduce the incidences of bullying and help children who are bullied learn strategies to reduce such incidents (see "Strategies for Children" on page 50). Adults can model assertive behaviors to support children who are bullied. Also, teaching children assertive phrases such as "Stop it" and "I don't like that" empowers them to stand up for themselves. Other methods include role-playing and teaching children to use I-messages. These messages consist of four parts: provide information, describe the effect, communicate how you feel, and state how to change things (Marion 2010). For example, children who are at risk of being bullied can learn to say, "When you tease me, it makes me sad and hurts my feelings. I want you to stop it, or I need to get help from an adult." In addition to *The Recess Queen* (see the opening vignette), *Stand Tall, Molly Lou Melon,* by Patty Lovell, illustrated by David Catrow (preschool–grade 2), features examples of assertive behavior.

Making sure that children know how to get adult help when they need it is crucial. To help children build self-esteem, adults can acknowledge their actions, ensure they know that a teacher is aware of the situation and is working to improve it, and make changes to accommodate them, if needed. Just listening to children and noting that you are aware of a situation lets them know that you care and want to help.

Reflection Questions

1. Family partnerships are a key to preventing and addressing bullying. Use recommendations from Chapter 7 in *Developmentally Appropriate Practice* (NAEYC 2022) to strengthen your relationships and reciprocal partnerships with families as an important way to prevent and address bullying.

2. As you plan your approaches to preventing and addressing bullying, consider ways in which bullying may especially target and affect children from historically marginalized groups.

3. Describe to a colleague or other partner one strategy you have used with children to encourage conversations about bullying situations. How effective was it?

4. With a colleague or other partner, share the title and a short summary of a children's book (one from this article or another favorite) that could be used to initiate a discussion with children about bullying. Consider children's ages, cultures, and developmental characteristics. Are there other resources (e.g., puppet stories, social stories) that might be used?

5. As the article discusses, the three most common forms of aggression in preschool are physical, instrumental, and relational. Which of these have you witnessed the most among young children? Did you intervene and, if so, how? Was it effective, and if not, what could you have done differently? For discussion of developmentally appropriate guidance strategies, see pages 117–119 in *Developmentally Appropriate Practice* (NAEYC 2022).

6. Does your school, program, or classroom have a policy on bullying? Do you consider the policy developmentally appropriate? Does the policy take into account children's developmental characteristics, positive collaboration strategies, and other important considerations?

7. At times, you and the families you work with may have different beliefs about bullying and may see different steps as appropriate in bullying situations. With a colleague or other partner, discuss (and, if possible, role-play) such an interaction with a family, taking into account the family's culture and context. As part of this communication exercise, review the information about practices and strategies that can build family partnerships on pages 147–152 in *Developmentally Appropriate Practice* (NAEYC 2022).

Strategies for Educators and Families

It is important for adults to use positive guidance that teaches young children how to make socially responsible choices (Gartrell & Gartrell 2008). It is also important to acknowledge positive behaviors, especially progress toward use of nonaggressive, assertive actions. For example, a preschooler enters her classroom and says, "This classroom is stupid." The teacher responds, "I am so happy to hear you using your words! Would you like to share with me what you don't like?" The parent looks surprised at the teacher's response and even more surprised when the child walks over to chat with the teacher. Adults can model positive behaviors. When the teacher listens to the child's comment, acknowledges the use of words as progress, and offers to discuss the child's feelings, she is modeling appropriate behavior for the child. Preschool teachers can significantly reduce the amount of bullying in their classrooms by implementing prosocial behavior strategies, modeling kindness and respect, teaching assertive skills, and creating a safe environment for children. Families can initiate discussions about bullying and actively listen to their children's responses.

It is also important to study the roles in the bullying process played by other students. If we think of the child who demonstrates bullying behavior and the child who is on the receiving end as playing social roles in the drama of bullying, then other students are the audience. Recognizing that any individual act of victimization has a third party (i.e., the audience) can facilitate a preventively focused, school-wide model of education that addresses the impact of misuses of power relationships between students (Twemlow et al. 2001).

Conclusion

At an early age, children can learn to consider the perspectives and feelings of other people. Often, bullying behavior can be prevented or reduced through teaching young children to respect others and be assertive. It is our responsibility to model socially appropriate behaviors and guide children along the journey to becoming responsible citizens.

REFERENCES

Ahmed, E. 2008. "'Stop It, That's Enough': Bystander Intervention and Its Relationship to School Connectedness and Shame Management." *Vulnerable Children and Youth Studies* 3 (3): 203–13.

Dodge, K.A., & N.R. Crick. 1990. "Social Information-Processing Bases of Aggressive Behavior in Children." *Personality and Social Psychology Bulletin* 16 (1): 8–22.

Freedman, J.S. 1999. "Easing the Teasing: How Parents Can Help Their Children." ERIC Digest. Champaign, IL: ERIC Clearinghouse on Elementary and Early Childhood Education.

Gartrell, D., & J.J. Gartrell. 2008. "Understand Bullying." Guidance Matters. *Young Children* 63 (3): 54–57.

Lacina, J., & R. Stetson. 2013. "Using Children's Literature to Support Positive Behaviors." *Young Children* 68 (5): 34–41.

Macintyre, C. 2009. *Bullying and Young Children: Understanding the Issues and Tackling the Problem.* New York: Routledge.

Marion, M.C. 2010. *Guidance of Young Children.* 8th ed. Upper Saddle River, NJ: Merrill/Prentice Hall.

NAEYC. 2022. *Developmentally Appropriate Practice in Early Childhood Programs Serving Children from Birth Through Age 8.* 4th ed. Washington, DC: NAEYC.

Olweus, D. 2003. "A Profile of Bullying at School." *Educational Leadership* 60 (6): 12–17.

Ostrov, J.M., K.E. Woods, E.A. Jansen, J.F. Casas, & N.R. Crick. 2004. "An Observational Study of Delivered and Received Aggression, Gender, and Social-Psychological Adjustment in Preschool: 'This White Crayon Doesn't Work . . .'" *Early Childhood Research Quarterly* 19 (2): 355–71.

Paley, V.G. 1992. *You Can't Say You Can't Play.* Cambridge, MA: Harvard University Press.

Piaget, J., & B. Inhelder. 1967. *The Child's Conception of Space.* Trans. F.J. Langdon & J.L. Lunzer. New York: Norton.

Twemlow, S.W., P. Fonagy, F. Sacco, M. Gies, & D. Hess. 2001. "Improving the Social and Intellectual Climate in Elementary Schools by Addressing Bully-Victim-Bystander Power Struggles." In *Caring Classrooms/Intelligent Schools: The Social Emotional Education of Young Children,* ed. J. Cohen, 162–182. New York: Teachers College Press.

About the Authors

Jill M. Raisor, PhD, is an associate professor in the Department of Teacher Education at the University of Southern Indiana. Her research focus is on social and emotional development, relational aggression, play, and developmentally appropriate practice.

Stacy D. Thompson, PhD, is a professor in the School of Education at Southern Illinois University. Her research interests include feeding young children, interventions for families and caregivers, and quality care for young children.

Never Too Young to Champion a Cause

Supporting Positive Identity Development Through Social Justice Curriculum in Preschool

Veronica Benavides, Roxanne Ledda, and Maimuna Mohammed

At the Garden of Learning and Discovery (GoLD) Pre-K Center in Highbridge, Bronx, we have chosen to focus on instilling a sense of social responsibility and advocacy into our teaching to enhance children's learning and development. Our belief is that we must go beyond the current status quo to drastically change outcomes for our most marginalized students; we also believe that our children are never too young to champion a cause. Because disparities in school performance can often be traced back to early childhood, growing appreciably during the primary and middle school years (Grodsky et al. 2017; Heckman 2011), we embraced a pedagogical stance that focuses on social justice, that is knowledge-rich, and that promotes positive identity development. It is leading to fundamental changes within the district, which "since 2010 . . . has been the poorest . . . House district in the country" (Santiago 2019).

In this article, we provide a look into our community and the contexts in which young children are growing and learning. Then, we describe our journey toward social justice advocacy and the process through which we developed a knowledge-rich curriculum to support positive identity development of our students and our beloved Highbridge community.

The Highbridge Community

In 2015, a New York City mayoral initiative led to more than triple the amount of prekindergarten spots available to NYC students and families. To meet this need, the GoLD Pre-K Center opened its doors as the sole Community School District 9 stand-alone center in Highbridge, Bronx. Highbridge is located in NYC Community District 4, and its residents are 96 percent families of color. While our community contends with a plethora of long-standing, systemic issues impacting quality of living (high levels of homelessness, minimal quality nutritional sources, and increased levels of disease), we found strength in concentrating on our communal cultures that are inclusive of resiliency and social capital. From a strengths-based perspective, we were able to "challenge inequity and disrupt unfair circumstances and situations" (Howard 2018, 28). We understood that we could not ameliorate all these structural inequities immediately, but we came to the conclusion that promoting justice and knowledge in our youngest learners (and ourselves) could lead to lasting and deep community engagement, empowerment, and evolution.

Our Journey into a Social Justice and Knowledge-Rich Curriculum

Our journey began in the fall of 2018, when GoLD partnered with the Center on Culture, Race & Equity (CCRE) at Bank Street College of Education. The CCRE and our staff embarked on a yearlong professional development series that guided our staff's learning about knowledge-rich curriculum, families as partners, culturally responsive practices, and children's identity development. This work resulted in our staff having a research-informed plan to engage students and families in a critical discussion about social justice and advocacy.

Knowledge-Rich Curriculum

In exploring aspects of knowledge-rich curriculum, we examined the interdependent relationship between concepts, content, knowledge, and skills. For example, we looked at how a lesson on water could be used to build knowledge of history, science, geography, art, literacy, social justice, and music. Through intentional curriculum mapping and careful planning of activities like read alouds, we learned to support our students in deepening their critical thinking skills and knowledge base.

In exploring the possibilities of a knowledge-rich curriculum, we also discussed the importance of teaching subject knowledge that foregrounds social justice. The knowledge we introduce to students should be powerful, equipping students to liberate themselves. According to Robertson (2016, n.p.), "any young person needs knowledge to thrive, and there is no reason why it can't sit alongside their own

culture, their own identity, non-elite stories, and knowledge." He goes on to state, "a radical curriculum would be knowledge-rich, and would leave its students empowered by the knowledge they were taught at school, not perplexed, years later, as to why nobody thought to introduce them to it while they were at school."

Families as Partners

As we participated in this professional development, we gained insights into what the research showed about positive, reciprocal partnerships with families. We learned

> Authentic home-school partnerships result in better student performance, healthier behavior, fewer behavior problems, and higher levels of enjoyment in school (The Fatherhood Project 2015).

> "School life should grow gradually out of [family] life, [and] it is the business of the school to deepen and extend the child's sense of values bound up in [their family] life" (Mooney 2010, 5).

> Authentic family engagement is a cornerstone of culturally responsive teaching (Bennett et al. 2018).

Equipped with this perspective, GoLD committed to enhancing an already-strong foundation of family engagement. We sought to engage the families of our students and the entire Highbridge community that surrounds and supports our youngest learners.

Culturally Responsive Practices

Our yearlong studying also revealed key elements of culturally responsive practices, including the following:

> Culturally responsive practices that use families' funds of knowledge as educational assets to help children learn (Gonzalez 2010). Integrating funds of knowledge, or the cultural assets of children's home lives, into school-based learning experiences means understanding and applying a strengths-based lens to each child and their family. Furthermore, using funds of knowledge and multiple modes of communication and learning can enhance educators' efforts to engage and empower families.

> Partnerships with local organizations devoted to social justice initiatives that serve the communities of students and their families in specific ways. These organizations can help to target issues and promote solutions that are in conjunction with the desires, perspectives, and assets of the community.

> Curriculum that places importance on text drawing from minoritized cultural and linguistic capitals might be used to empower students in different ways; not only encouraging "their identity investment in this learning, but also to shift the balance of authority and expertise among teachers, students, and families" (Taylor et al. 2008, 272).

In order to deeply understand and internalize the tenets of culturally responsive practice, we began by exploring our own cultural practices and norms, including from "the positions of privilege we occupy—such as being White, having grown up in an economically comfortable household, speaking Mainstream American English, being heterosexual, or being Christian" (Souto-Manning 2013, 12). Once we understood more about our positions of privilege and cultural identities, we could more deeply explore how our own upbringings and experiences influence the classroom and school climate, the content taught, and the methods used at GoLD. Certain research helped guide us to examine the impact of White middle-class norms on school culture and standards, for example:

When students of color are rewarded (or sometimes chastised) for conformity to white norms and standards, whiteness becomes an alienable property. This can specifically be seen in what is often referred to as students "acting white," or in depictions of Asian Americans as "model minorities," because they adhere to an array of characteristics endorsed by white society and attributed to whiteness. (Rector-Aranda 2016, 7)

Too often, schools have sought to prepare students for the "real world," stripping away cultural assets that could support children in navigating and thriving in life (a second language or code-switching). In examining the origins and functions of typical academic standards for "success," GoLD peeled back the layers of deeply ingrained schoolwide cultural beliefs and sought to create a learning environment that nurtured and built upon the existing cultural assets of our students and families.

According to Robin DiAngelo (2016), "*minoritized* [refers to] a social group that is devalued in society. This devaluing encompasses how the group is represented, what degree of access to resources it is granted, and how the unequal access is rationalized. The term *minoritized* (rather than minority) is used to indicate that the group's lower position is a function of active socially constructed dynamics, rather than its numbers in society" (82).

Identity Development in Early Childhood

Finally, our yearlong professional development included research about identity development, and we learned

> Children develop conceptions of race at a young age, beginning with knowledge of color categories, to a conceptual awareness of racial categories, to ultimately an awareness of group identity (Farago, Davidson, & Byrd 2019; Swanson et al. 2009).

> Understanding oneself is inexplicably tied to understanding where one fits into a group (Baldwin et al. 1991).

> The concept of "stereotype threat" is about "being at risk of confirming, as a self-characteristic, a negative stereotype about one's group" (Steele & Aronson 1995, 797) and about its impact on the academic performance of students of color. For example, the threat that the judgements of others or their own actions would negatively stereotype them resulted in underperformance of Black participants taking a standardized test.

> Children as young as 5 years of age are susceptible to stereotype threat—predicting, for example, that an Asian student would outperform a White student on a math exam (Ambady et al. 2001).

> A child's sense of self is correlated with the development of cognitive and noncognitive abilities and academic outcomes (Ladson-Billings 2009). Too often, the stereotypes of children from minoritized communities shape their feelings of academic inferiority and uncertainty about whether they belong (Walton & Cohen 2011), adversely impacting their motivation to learn.

Based on this research, we knew that our children at GoLD would learn best with the confidence that they belong in our learning community and have a voice and agency here. While we believed that most of our children felt a sense of belonging, we dove deep into questions about identity and belongingness for children who stood outside of the margins; we wanted to ensure that, at GoLD, all of the children felt included, represented, and empowered in our center, including children whose social identities are not typically reflected in school.

We emerged from our time of study and reflection with a new and deeper understanding of families as partners, knowledge-rich curriculum within the context of culturally responsive practices, and children's identity development. However, there are few examples of developmentally appropriate approaches that address all of these areas of the curriculum and learning environment. For that reason, GoLD decided to develop a school-wide social justice project to support children's positive identity development through a knowledge-rich curriculum, outlined in the following section.

Seeds of Change: A Social Justice, Knowledge-Rich Approach

With the understanding that identity-affirming spaces for our children and families contribute to positive child outcomes, the Seeds of Change Initiative was born. GoLD's Seeds of Change Initiative aimed to build individual and collective agency amongst children by bringing awareness to the local and global health crisis affecting our community. Children researched and actively contributed to the creation of practical solutions to local and global challenges. Our goal was to positively connect with

and support our families and bring wakefulness to micro- and macro-instances of environmental and social injustices. We began by exploring the nutritional deficiencies present within the community of Highbridge, and we decided that we had to address the lack of affordable and nutritional food options.

To launch our Seeds of Change Initiative, we organized a planting party for our community. Over half of the families of our students attended the planting party, and many of them led the organization of the event, supported the event with food donation, offered assistance with program design, and provided translation of materials. At the planting party, families discussed their own experiences with environmental injustice and learned about ways they could support their children in making a difference. Families and children took their first step in making change by painting pots and planting seeds for the indoor garden. Through this initiative, GoLD was able to strengthen a sense of belonging, engagement, and activism amongst children and families.

Based on the energy of our launch event, GoLD inaugurated a wide-ranging edible indoor garden in May 2019 to supplement the nutritional and physical needs of our community. As our students learned about their community and themselves through themes such as "My Community and Me" and "5 Senses," they expanded their ever-changing palates by learning how fresh food is planted, grown, cultivated, distributed, and prepared. They also learned about their place within a local and global community. They learned about how they have a role to play in the larger environmental ecosystem.

We did not stop our transformative change project there. GoLD understood that we needed to integrate social justice practices into our thematic units throughout the school year as a way to expand and enrich our curriculum. We decided to introduce global issues such as water accessibility and conservation by holding informative sessions for families and participating in a whole-school, reusable water bottle challenge. Our desire was to raise awareness about the scarcity of water throughout our international communities, making sure our children knew that there are 3-, 4- and 5-year-olds that have to walk miles every single day for a luxury our students just had to turn the faucet to obtain. As the students became more knowledgeable of the factors that plagued others, we began to see an increase in the level of empathy shown toward their peers and a desire to bring change to their community as a whole.

The GoLD Walk for Water

On June 12, 2019, GoLD concluded the first year of our social justice, knowledge-rich approach to teaching and learning with a televised Walk for Water. Joined by our students, staff, families, and community members, we walked across the High Bridge, a historical aqueduct that once transported water between Manhattan and the Bronx, to bring awareness to the global water crisis. To further contextualize why we were embarking on this Walk for Water and what it meant in a global context, the school partnered with the We Movement, a social activism organization who contends that more than 840 million people worldwide are living without access to clean water and 40 percent of the world's population is affected by water scarcity. As we walked and chanted on that June afternoon, our community supported us with cheerful applause and genuine surprise and delight at the thunder of preschoolers' feet that passed their buildings. At that moment, the students at GoLD joined the ranks of other young social justice organizers in history, totaling 90 4- to 5-year-olds participating. The GoLD Walk for Water was a culmination of months of introspection, transformative change, and conservation efforts. One community member reflected, "The children may be small, but their message is big!" A GoLD teacher commented, "The transformation in engagement and agency is clear. Kids are never too young to learn about activism. Our children now know their voices matter and that they can make a difference."

Reflecting Back and Looking Ahead

This process of collective investigation and action allowed us to further support children in critically understanding their identity and how it intersects with the world. They were able to see themselves as authors of their own narrative, empowered to create change in the face of challenge. Looking back at the four key elements learned during our professional development work, we found that they, indeed, contributed to our success in implementing this social justice advocacy process.

Reflection Questions

1. The article authors state that "our children are never too young to champion a cause." Reflect on this belief. Do you agree or disagree with it, and on what basis?

2. The article describes a staff's professional development work focused on social justice through knowledge-rich curriculum, close partnerships with families, and culturally responsive practices. What aspects of this work have you seen (or would be feasible) in the context of your early learning setting?

3. Consistent with this article, *Developmentally Appropriate Practice* (NAEYC 2022) emphasizes the importance of teachers developing an understanding of children's contexts and cultural assets (in particular, see pages 18–22), as well as teachers' reflection on their own contexts. With a colleague or other partner, engage in dialogue about your contexts, your colleague's contexts, and the contexts of the children you teach. How might you begin to deepen your knowledge?

4. With a colleague or other partner, brainstorm some ideas for a project or event like the Walk for Water that aims to build children's commitment to community change and increase their empathy for others.

5. A theme in this article is the importance of supporting each child's positive identity development. As described in *Developmentally Appropriate Practice* (NAEYC 2022), children's identities provide them with feelings of pride, self-worth, and belonging. With a colleague or other partner, examine the identity development of several children—its sources, its characteristics, and what you do and can do to strengthen it.

Knowledge-Rich Curriculum

Through this project, we were able to enhance the impact of existing curriculum through culturally responsive practice. Children talked about the role of food and water in their lives and communities. They learned about the process of recycling through creating usable recycling systems for their community. This interdisciplinary approach enhanced engagement and impact for our youngest learners.

Authentic Family Engagement

New York City has the largest school district in the United States, as well as the most rapidly evolving, diverse demographic groups of student populations (National Center for Education Statistics, n.d.). It is important for educators to appreciate what each child brings to their school and how these experiences can be used to foster learning and inform instruction. This project would not have been successful without this support and investment from GoLD families. They dedicated their time, expertise, and resources to creating transformative experiences for the children and community.

Community Partnerships

In addition to family engagement, GoLD sought out community partnerships to support the innovative work of our school community. Our partnerships with CCRE and the We Movement allowed us to think outside of the box and utilize existing funds of knowledge to create transformative change in our community. These outside partnerships not only introduced new ideas and concepts to inspire action, but they also provided the critical thought-partnership needed to dream big and inspire action.

Understanding the Importance of Identity

Children form a sense of identity from an early age. Our students carry group identities across a range of categories: race, gender, age, and income. We know that children develop conceptions of race at a young age and this impacts their understanding of self and the world. Therefore, we decided to take an active role in helping to shape a positive identity through agency-enhancing, social justice curriculum. We want children to view themselves and their community as empowered agents of change in this world. Our young children can hold the complexity of two powerful ideas at the same time: sometimes unfair things exist in this world (there is a lack of access to healthy food options in our neighborhood) and we can make a difference and change things (we can build an indoor community garden).

Through this work, we realized that early childhood is the perfect time to begin the establishment of a collective and empathetic mindset. As stated earlier, our children are never too young to learn about activism and social justice. As early childhood educators, we need to introduce this work organically, to weave it throughout our instruction and interactions, and to ensure it is developmentally appropriate. At GoLD, we believe it is never too early to provide our youngest learners with the tools necessary to become environmental advocates and global ambassadors because we understand that this should be an integral part of what is learned in early childhood. A knowledge-rich and action-oriented education lays the foundation for an indestructible and more equitable society.

REFERENCES

Ambady, N., M. Shih, A. Kim, & T.L. Pittinsky. 2001. "Stereotype Susceptibility in Children: Effects of Identity Activation on Quantitative Performance." *Psychological Science* 12 (5): 385–390.

Baldwin, J.A., R. Brown, & R. Hopkins. 1991. "The Black Self-Hatred Paradigm Revisited: An Afrocentric Analysis." In *Black Psychology,* ed. R.L. Jones, 28–44. Berkeley, CA: Cobb & Henry.

Bennett, S.V., A.A. Gunn, G. Gayle-Evans, E.S. Barrera, & C.B. Leung. 2018. "Culturally Responsive Literacy Practices in an Early Childhood Community." *Early Childhood Education Journal* 46 (2): 241–48.

DiAngelo, R. 2016. *What Does It Mean to Be White? Developing White Racial Literacy.* New York: Peter Lang.

Farago, F., K.L. Davidson, & C.M. Byrd. 2019. "Ethnic-Racial Socialization in Early Childhood: The Implications of Color-Consciousness and Colorblindness for Prejudice Development." In *Handbook of Children and Prejudice,* eds. H.E. Fitzgerald, D.J. Johnson, D.B. Qin, F.A. Villarruel, & J. Norder, 131–45. Cham, Switzerland: Springer.

The Fatherhood Project. 2015. "4 Steps to Engaging Dads in Schools." *The Fatherhood Project,* August 17. www. thefatherhoodproject.org/4-steps-to-engaging-dads-in-schools.

Gonzalez, J. 2010. *50 Strategies for Communicating and Working with Diverse Families.* Boston: Pearson Education.

Grodsky, E., Y. Huangfu, H.R. Miesner, & C. Packard. 2017. "Kindergarten Readiness in Wisconsin." WCER Working Paper No. 2017-3. Madison, WI: University of Wisconsin–Madison, Wisconsin Center for Education Research. https://wcer.wisc. edu/docs/working-papers/Working_Paper_No_2017_3.pdf.

Heckman, J.J. 2011. "The Economics of Inequality: The Value of Early Childhood Education." *American Educator* 35 (1): 31.

Howard, T.C. 2018. "Capitalizing on Culture: Engaging Young Learners in Diverse Classrooms." *Young Children* 73 (2): 24–33.

Ladson-Billings, G. 2009. *The Dreamkeepers: Successful Teachers of African American Children.* San Francisco: Jossey-Bass.

Mooney, C. 2010. *Theories of Attachment: An Introduction to Bowlby, Ainsworth, Gerber, Brazelton, Kennell and Klaus.* St. Paul, MN: Redleaf Press.

NAEYC. 2022. *Developmentally Appropriate Practice in Early Childhood Programs Serving Children from Birth Through Age 8.* 4th ed. Washington, DC: NAEYC.

National Center for Education Statistics. n.d. "Largest School Districts in the United States by Enrollment." ELSI Table Generator from National Center for Education Statistics. https://nces.ed.gov/ccd/elsi.

Rector-Aranda, A. 2016. "School Norms and Reforms, Critical Race Theory, and the Fairytale of Equitable Education." *Critical Questions in Education* 7 (1).

Robertson, A. 2016. "The Radical Case for a Knowledge-Rich Curriculum." *Left History Teaching,* March 24. https://lefthistoryteaching.wordpress.com/2016/03/24/the-radical-case-for-a-knowledge-rich-curriculum.

Santiago, A. 2019. "NY Has the Richest, Poorest, Smallest, Most Unequal Congressional Districts." *City and State NY,* December 5. www.cityandstateny.com/articles/politics/new-york-state/ny-has-richest-poorest-smallest-most-unequal-congressional.

Souto-Manning, M. 2013. *Multicultural Teaching in the Early Childhood Classroom: Approaches, Strategies, and Tools, Preschool–2nd Grade.* New York: Teachers College Press.

Steele, C.M., & J. Aronson. 1995. "Stereotype Threat and the Intellectual Test Performance of African Americans." Journal of Personality and Social Psychology 69 (5): 797–811.

Swanson, D.P., M. Cunningham, J. Youngblood, & M.B. Spencer. 2009. "Racial Identity Development During Childhood." In *Handbook of African American Psychology,* eds. H.A. Neville, B.M. Tynes, & S.O. Utsey, 269–281. Thousand Oaks, CA: Sage.

Taylor, L.K., J.K. Bernhard, S. Garg, & J. Cummins. 2008. "Affirming Plural Belonging: Building on Students' Family-Based Cultural and Linguistic Capital Through Multiliteracies Pedagogy." *Journal of Early Childhood Literacy* 8 (3): 269–94.

Walton, G.M., & G.L. Cohen. 2011. "A Brief Social-Belonging Intervention Improves Academic and Health Outcomes of Minority Students." *Science* 331 (6023): 1447–51.

About the Authors

Veronica Benavides, EdLD, is passionate about building a more just and equitable world. She is an experienced educator, facilitator, change management strategist, and leadership development specialist. Dr. Benavides received her doctorate in education leadership from Harvard Graduate School of Education.

Roxanne Ledda, MSEd, MBA, is principal of The Max P.S. 70 elementary school, located in Bronx, New York. Formerly, she was director of early childhood in NYC CSD 9. Roxanne is committed to the provision of culturally responsive educational experiences for the youngest learners within the NYC school portfolio as well as ensuring that social justice project-based learning is integrated throughout the elementary school trajectory.

Maimuna Mohammed, MSEd, is an early childhood educational equity consultant and practitioner. She is an experienced diversity, equity, inclusion, and belonging (DEIB) content developer and facilitator. Maimuna has over 30 years of teaching experience and over 22 years of experience working as an early childhood educator in community-based programs in New York City.

Supporting Children and Families in Difficult Times

Individual children worry. Families struggle with poverty and trauma. Systemic biases impact communities. International conflicts prompt migration. A pandemic disrupts lives around the globe.

There seems to be no end to the challenges young children and their families face today. It is more important than ever to incorporate attention to these issues into discussions of the effects stress and trauma can have on children's development and learning (for example, see NAEYC 2022, 28, 113–115) and into practices that support children and their families as they encounter difficulties. Reciprocal partnerships with families help teachers identify individual, community, and cultural assets that can be drawn upon to foster children's sense of safety and security.

The four articles in this part describe challenges encountered by children, families, and communities, offering examples of interactions, learning environments, and activities to support children's social and emotional development during these experiences.

After summarizing research on the impact of trauma on the brain and behavior, **Katie Statman-Weil** provides specific suggestions for helping children who have experienced trauma in "Creating Trauma-Sensitive Classrooms." A primary emphasis of the article is the importance of loving and nurturing adults in mitigating the effects of trauma in children's lives.

"Supporting Anxious Children in the Preschool Classroom" begins by noting the heightened anxiety occasioned during the pandemic. **Sierra L. Brown, Allison Aberson, Stephanie Easley,** and **Kara E. McGoey** then offer a collection of strategies to relieve anxiety, teach coping skills, and help children move forward in social and emotional skill development.

In "Welcoming Refugee Children into Early Childhood Classrooms," **Sadia Warsi** describes ways that early childhood teachers can show respect for the experiences and cultural assets that children bring to their new environment. Experiences of stress and trauma, as well as the disruption of relocation, create emotional needs for many children; the author suggests how educators can meet those needs and help families feel like a valued part of the community.

Nature-based scavenger hunts, classroom gardens, classroom jobs caring for plants and animals, and other interactions with nature are explored as ways to manage anxiety and build competence in individualized, contextually appropriate ways in "Using Nature Contact to Support Children Under Stress," by **Becky L. DelVecchio, Susan Ferguson,** and **Wesley Knapp.**

REFERENCE

NAEYC. 2022. *Developmentally Appropriate Practice in Early Childhood Programs Serving Children from Birth Through Age 8.* 4th ed. Washington, DC: NAEYC.

Creating Trauma-Sensitive Classrooms

Katie Statman-Weil

Four-year-old Alex is in his first year of preschool. He loves his teachers and is always excited to come to school, yet his teachers describe his behavior as "out of control." At times he screams, curses at his classmates and teachers, and destroys classroom materials and other children's artwork—all seemingly without cause. Unbeknownst to his teachers, Alex has been witnessing domestic violence and experiencing physical abuse since birth. Furthermore, Alex's mom works the night shift and his dad works the day shift at the same 24-hour diner. Because of his parents' schedules, there are times when Alex wakes in the morning and finds himself home alone.

Chiara, a 7-year-old second-grader, was sexually abused between the ages of 2 and 4 by her teenage cousin. Chiara is clearly a bright child but is falling behind academically even though she never misses a day of school. In class she spends most of her time daydreaming. On the playground she has a hard time initiating play with her peers, so she tends to play with younger children. In an effort to determine the best way to help Chiara, her teacher, Ms. Martinez, consults with Chiara's first grade teacher, who had been equally perplexed by Chiara's behavior. Neither teacher is aware that withdrawal can be a symptom of abuse.

Alex and Chiara are just two examples of the numerous young children who have experienced early trauma. Roughly 26 percent of children in the United States witness or experience a trauma before the age of 4 (Briggs-Gowan et al. 2010). In 2015, an estimated 683,000 children were victims of child abuse and neglect. More than half of all victims (63.8 percent) were between birth and 8 years old. More than one quarter (27.7 percent) were younger than 3 years old, 18.6 percent were between the ages of 3 and 5, and another 17.5 percent were between the ages of 6 and 8. Almost 80 percent of these early traumas occurred at home and were perpetrated by the children's own parents (HHS 2015).

Many early childhood educators are likely to encounter young children who have experienced trauma on a daily basis. These traumas may include emotional, physical, or sexual abuse; domestic violence; various forms of neglect; adoption; foster care; incarceration or death of a caregiver; natural disasters; medical and surgical procedures; and serious accidents (Herman [1992] 1997; NCTSNSC 2008; van der Kolk 2005). Contemporary trauma research demonstrates that all types of trauma can undermine children's abilities to learn, create healthy attachments, form supportive relationships, and follow classroom expectations (NCTSNSC 2008). Further, trauma has negative behavioral, emotional, neurobiological, and developmental repercussions throughout children's schooling and their adult lives. Children who experience trauma are two-and-a-half times more likely to fail a grade in school than their nontraumatized peers. They score lower on standardized tests, have higher rates of suspension and expulsion, and are more likely to be placed in special education classrooms rather than be included in classrooms with their nontraumatized peers (Cole et al. 2013; NCTSNSC 2008).

A significant number of children experience trauma, and the effects can be profound. It is imperative, therefore, that early childhood settings be safe, trauma-sensitive spaces where teachers support children in creating positive self-identities. A foundation in trauma research and response can help educators optimally support all children—including those whose traumas have been documented, those whose traumas have not been formally recognized, and those who might be affected by their classmates' traumas (Cole et al. 2013).

Feeling positive and confident about school in the early years is important for children. Early on, children decide whether they view themselves as learners, and by age 8 most children are on the academic path they will follow throughout their schooling (Stacks & Oshio 2009). To best support

Meeting the Needs of Families Whose Children May Have Experienced Trauma

Signs and symptoms of early childhood trauma can be easily mistaken for those of other developmental issues, such as attention-deficit/hyperactivity disorder or autism spectrum disorder. If a child receives a wrong diagnosis, or if symptoms are explained away as simply rowdiness or attention difficulties, the child may not get the support needed to overcome a traumatic experience. Therefore, it is important for educators to work closely with families to ensure children receive the help and support they need. Here are some ways to work with families and outside specialists.

> Engage and include families in the program or school in caring, nonjudgmental ways—hold regularly scheduled meetings, invite them to the classroom to volunteer, and correspond through email and telephone. Use these opportunities with families to deepen your connection by learning more about their home lives and offering space for them to ask questions about the program.

> If a child is working with an outside specialist (such as a trauma specialist or a child therapist), ask for the family's permission to invite the specialist to the classroom so that you can collaborate to better support the child.

> Work with both specialists and families to create Individualized Family Service Plans, Individualized Education Programs, or Individual Support Plans that support children's positive behaviors, development, and learning, and promote caregiver responsiveness (CEC 2009).

If you have reason to suspect child abuse or neglect, report the suspected maltreatment to the appropriate state agency.

young children, teachers must understand the influence of early attachment patterns and the neurobiology of the early years. This knowledge can help teachers to have patience and compassion for all children—especially in the children's most challenging times.

The Impact of Trauma on Attachment and the Brain

Children's brains develop in the context of their earliest experiences; their neural development and social interactions are inextricably interconnected (Badenoch 2008; van der Kolk 2005). Young children learn how to self-regulate by anticipating their parents' and teachers' responses to them when they express various emotions. Children who have secure attachments learn to trust their emotions and their understanding of the world around them (Stacks & Oshio 2009; Stubenbort, Cohen, & Trybalski 2010). Children's early experiences of feeling listened to and understood help instill confidence in their ability to make good things happen and to seek out individuals who can support them in finding a solution when they do not know how to handle a difficult situation (Porges 2004; van der Kolk 2005).

Typically, when children experience distress or feel threatened, parents or other caregivers support them in reestablishing a sense of safety and control. In contrast, children who experience early trauma at the hands of such trusted adults may not have the experiences that lead to healthy attachments, such as adult guidance to help them regulate their emotions and physical reactions to stressful events. Children's inability to access the support they need during a stressful situation can interrupt their ability to process, integrate, and categorize what happened. This leaves young trauma survivors at risk for being overwhelmed by feelings of distress and unable to regulate their internal emotional and physical states, such as heart rate and breathing (van der Kolk 2005).

Brain research shows that when children encounter a perceived threat to their physical or mental safety, their brains trigger a set of chemical and neurological reactions—known as the *stress response*—which activates their biological instinct to fight, freeze, or flee (Porges 2004; Wright 2014). Experiencing trauma in the early years can cause the stress response to become highly reactive or difficult to end when there is a perceived threat. Chronic stress or fear raises both the cortisol and adrenaline hormone levels in young children, which can cause them to be in a state of hyperarousal—constantly on guard. This continuous fear, which can make them vulnerable to anxiety, panic, hypervigilance, and increased heart rate, can also inhibit their higher-level thinking (Koplow & Ferber 2007; Siegel 2012).

When Alex's stress response is triggered by an event or sensation—a toy dropping loudly or a child pretending to be a crying baby during dramatic play—it reminds him of a traumatic experience, and his body responds as if he is experiencing the trauma all over again. He has a physiological reaction appropriate for a serious threat, which inhibits him from being able to use the higher, more complex area of his brain to recognize that the loud noise of the toy dropping surprised him or that the baby crying was just pretend. Alex screams and yells in class because the trigger causes him to reexperience the stress response, which mimics his response during a trauma (Koomar 2009; Koplow & Ferber 2007; Siegel 2012).

For children living with trauma, the stress response can become their regular manner of functioning (Wolpow et al. 2009). The areas of children's brains that become the most developed are those that are most frequently activated and used (Badenoch 2008). When children live in a constant state of fear and are not supported in the regulation of their emotions, the *amygdala* (the brain's regulator of emotions and emotional behaviors) tends to be overused, causing it to overdevelop. This can result in children being highly impulsive and reactive and unable to complete higher-level thinking tasks.

Conversely, the *hippocampus*—the part of the brain that puts a potential threat in context—tends to be underdeveloped in children who experience trauma because it is underused (van der Kolk 2003). Therefore, even when the dangers they have experienced are not present, children who have experienced trauma may respond as if they are in danger because the hippocampus is unable to override the stress response their brains so frequently employ as a means of survival (van der Kolk 2003; Wolpow et al. 2009). Many of the behaviors of such children can be understood as their efforts to minimize perceived threats and regulate emotional distress.

Expressions of Trauma in Early Childhood Settings

The behaviors of childhood trauma survivors can often frustrate and overwhelm teachers. Children may have impairments across the developmental domains—physical, cognitive, social and emotional, and language and literacy—that manifest as challenging and troubling behaviors in the classroom (Koomar 2009). These children's external behaviors are often confusing because they are instigated by internal processes that the children themselves most likely do not completely understand and that teachers cannot observe or infer (Koplow & Ferber 2007; van der Kolk 2005).

A child who has survived trauma may experience delays and challenging behaviors in the following areas.

Language and Communication

Early trauma can undermine the development of linguistic and communication skills, which in turn hinders the important social and emotional regulation necessary for school success (Wolpow et al. 2009). For example, when children spend their early years exposed primarily to *instrumental language*—language that is used to direct and command behavior ("Sit down," "Come here," "Be quiet")—they may not be equipped with the language needed to express thoughts and feelings in social interactions (Cole et al. 2013). Alex, who primarily experiences instrumental language at home, uses that same language in the classroom, appearing demanding and inflexible. He lacks the language to communicate empathy or to problem solve because the important adults in his life do not use it.

Social and Emotional Regulation

Many children who survive trauma may have a difficult time regulating their emotions. Like Alex, they are often overwhelmed by feelings of fear and stress that keep their brains in a state of hyperarousal. The inability to self-regulate can present itself in the classroom or other learning settings as being unable to control impulses; behaving aggressively toward oneself or others; misunderstanding or being unable to identify other people's facial and body expressions; and feeling unsure about the security

Suggestions for Helping Children Who Have Experienced Trauma

Not all strategies work for all children. While a calming pat on the back may work well when Alex is feeling upset, this may have the opposite effect on Chiara and cause her to retreat further into herself. Find strengths even in children with the most challenging behaviors, and remind them often of what they are doing well (Wolpow et al. 2009). Here are some ways to help children who have experienced trauma.

Create and maintain consistent daily routines for the classroom. Stability helps children understand that the world can be a safe place (NCTSNSC 2008). They feel empowered when they know the order of events and how they will be carried out. For example, placing a visual calendar on a wall or creating a book with images outlining the daily schedule for the library center can help children like Alex and Chiara feel more in control of their experiences.

Tell children when something out of the ordinary is going to occur. The smallest unexpected event—such as a loud noise or a visit from an outsider—can be a reminder of trauma and trigger children's stress responses; therefore, it is important to try to mitigate the fear and uncertainty that often come with unexpected changes (van der Kolk 2005).

For example, during a study of trees Alex's teachers invite a park ranger to talk to the children. Three days before the park ranger's visit, the teachers hold a class meeting to discuss the upcoming visit and answer the children's questions about the ranger. The teachers let the children express their feelings and concerns about a stranger coming into the classroom. By the time the ranger arrives, the children have agreed on how they will introduce themselves to their guest and some of the questions they will ask. This helps Alex feel less fearful of the new person and allows him to grapple with some of his fears outside of the trauma scenario.

Offer children developmentally appropriate choices. Traumatic events often involve loss of control. Empowering children to have ownership of their behaviors and interests by giving them choices about things like where they want to sit at lunch or which songs to sing at circle time can help build healthy self-esteem (NCTSNSC 2008).

Anticipate difficult periods and transitions during the school day and offer extra support during these times. Many different situations can remind children of their traumas, but your support can help to alleviate their responses. Because Alex finds himself alone in the house when he wakes up some mornings, he may feel anxious during naptime and have trouble falling asleep. Rather than resting, he might watch the teacher to make sure she stays in the room. To support him, the teacher sits by Alex while he falls asleep and reminds him that she will not leave him alone (Perry & Szalavitz 2006).

of their relationships. Learning the skills to regulate feelings or modulate emotions is an important predictor of school and social success (Streeck-Fischer & van der Kolk 2000; Stubenbort, Cohen, & Trybalski 2010).

Building Relationships

Children who have not been exposed regularly to words and phrases that allow them to identify and express their feelings may struggle to interact successfully with peers and teachers. Young children who have difficulty connecting and relating to their peers tend to experience ongoing social difficulties throughout their schooling. When children's early experiences have been unsafe and unstable, keeping others at a distance is a way to emotionally, and sometimes physically, protect themselves.

Use techniques to support children's self-regulation. Introducing breathing and other centering activities, such as mindfulness, helps children self-regulate (Perry & Szalavitz 2006). Starting off each day with a special breathing ritual gives them the strategy they need to pay attention and to modify their breaths when they are stressed.

Understand that children make sense of their experiences by reenacting them in play or through interactions with peers or adults. Alex's teacher rings the bell to initiate cleanup time. Alex asks if he can get out the clay. The teacher says it is not an appropriate time and points to the bell as she explains that it is time to clean up and get ready to go home for the day. Alex becomes visibly upset and yells "I hate you!" before running into the corner and banging his head against the wall.

Teachers can help children like Alex to manage their feelings during such experiences by remaining composed and offering empathy and support. Rather than becoming the angry adult Alex expects, the teacher calmly initiates healthy and reparative interactions. She validates Alex's feelings and communicates that she understands that Alex is upset. She also explains to Alex that she needs to keep his body safe and slowly moves her body between Alex and the wall so that he can no longer bang his head (NCTSNSC 2008). With the teacher's support, Alex is able to calm down. Before joining his peers for cleanup, Alex makes a plan with the teacher to bring the clay out the next day.

Be nurturing and affectionate but also sensitive to children's individual triggers. Chiara's history of sexual abuse causes her to feel anxious and confused when her teachers hug her. Being physically close to young children can reassure them, but with Chiara, a good rule of thumb is to be physically affectionate only when she seeks it. The teacher asks Chiara whether she wants to be hugged, and if she does, the teacher holds and hugs her (Perry & Szalavitz 2006).

Use positive guidance to help all children. Strive to create supportive interventions to guide children to appropriate activities. For example, when Alex rips up his classmate Juan's artwork, the teacher helps him understand that his actions upset Juan, and she encourages Alex to help repair Juan's artwork. This enables Alex to connect his actions to his peer's feelings while creating the expectation that he repair the physical damage he causes (Fox & Hemmeter 2009).

Like Alex, children who have experienced trauma may engage in dangerous behaviors or use hurtful language. Alex swears and yells epithets at his teachers and the other children as an unconscious means of protecting himself from forming relationships that could potentially cause pain or harm. He creates barriers to relationships and emotional distance between himself and others to protect himself from further injury (Cole et al. 2013).

Play

Trauma can interfere with some children's capacities for imaginative and creative play—important ways young children build the cognitive, physical, and social and emotional skills necessary for later school success (Ginsburg 2007). Through play, young children learn how others experience the world and how to develop control and competence to deal with scary feelings, individuals, and circumstances (Streeck-Fischer & van der Kolk 2000). Children who have experienced trauma may not develop these skills because the feelings that arise during play may overwhelm them. Children without trauma backgrounds tend to be assertive in initiating play and can solve conflicts that arise during their play.

Chiara, who has lived through trauma, has difficulty initiating play with children her age. She tends to engage with younger children because her play skills, reflective of her general interpersonal skills, are below the level typical for a child her age (Stubenbort, Cohen, & Trybalski 2010). Further, Chiara often initiates game scenarios in which her play partners instruct her to do something she doesn't want to do (such as sit in time-out or clean her room). Through this experience she is reliving the experiences of not being able to say no to her cousin when she was sexually abused. Rather than creating different outcomes in her play, perhaps where she refuses her cousin or an adult comes to help her, Chiara complies with the request. This causes her stress response to activate as if she is back in the traumatic experience. Thus, her play leads to repeating the traumatic feelings rather than allowing her to escape into her imagination, as such play does for children who are not traumatized (Streeck-Fischer & van der Kolk 2000; Stubenbort, Cohen, & Trybalski 2010).

Withdrawal

Children who have experienced early trauma may have a hard time listening and concentrating in class because they dissociate or freeze when their stress responses are triggered by sounds, smells, or behaviors that remind them of the trauma. Chiara tends to dissociate if someone touches her when she does not expect it, even when it is meant as a friendly touch, such as a pat on the back. The teacher does not recognize this behavior as dissociation and instead views Chiara as a daydreamer. She often goes unnoticed in the classroom because when her stress response is triggered, rather than make a loud commotion, Chiara silently withdraws into herself. Chiara's so-called daydreaming—her withdrawal behavior—leaves her as vulnerable to falling behind academically as Alex's aggression and acting out do (Cole et al. 2013).

Supporting Children Who Have Experienced Trauma

These manifestations of early childhood trauma—difficulties learning, playing, communicating, interacting, and creating relationships—can exasperate teachers and reinforce children's negative self-images. These behavioral symptoms of children surviving trauma are often misunderstood and viewed as intentional and controlled acts or as diagnosable disorders not specifically related to trauma, such as oppositional defiant disorder or attention-deficit/hyperactivity disorder, rather than as symptoms of trauma (van der Kolk 2005). To fully understand children's challenging behaviors, it is imperative that teachers communicate with children's families regularly to understand whether the behaviors seen in the classroom might be connected to traumatic experiences (Wright 2014).

Resources for Information About Childhood Trauma

> **National Child Traumatic Stress Network (NCTSN):** www.nctsn.org

> **Child Trauma Academy (CTA):** www.childtrauma.org

> **Trauma Center at Justice Resource Institute:** www.traumacenter.org

> **National Institute for Trauma and Loss in Children (TLC):** https://starr.org/programs/national-institute-for-trauma-and-loss-in-children-tlc

> **Reporting child abuse and neglect:** www.childwelfare.gov/topics/responding/reporting/how

More than anything, children who have survived trauma need loving and nurturing adults who can support them in their most troubling moments. Children's brains have the ability to change and reorganize in response to new experiences; therefore, having healthy and consistent interactions with early childhood educators can greatly influence their brain development and their ability to engage successfully in the early childhood setting (Cole et al. 2013). (For specific ways to support young children who have experienced trauma, see "Suggestions for Helping Children Who Have Experienced Trauma" on pages 68–69.)

Conclusion

In the end, what matters most in helping young children process and cope with physical, emotional, and psychological trauma is having important adults whom children trust and rely on to offer them unconditional love, support, and encouragement. Through our own actions, we early childhood professionals can have a powerful influence on mitigating the effects of trauma experienced by children like Chiara and Alex by being loving, safe, and consistent caregivers and educators.

REFERENCES

Badenoch, B. 2008. *Being a Brain-Wise Therapist: A Practical Guide to Interpersonal Neurobiology.* New York: Norton.

Briggs-Gowan, M.J., J.D. Ford, L. Fraleigh, K. McCarthy, & A.S. Carter. 2010. "Prevalence of Exposure to Potentially Traumatic Events in a Healthy Birth Cohort of Very Young Children in the Northeastern United States." *Journal of Traumatic Stress* 23 (6): 725–33.

CEC (Council for Exceptional Children). 2009. *What Every Special Educator Must Know: Ethics, Standards, and Guidelines.* 6th ed. rev. Arlington, VA: CEC.

Cole, S.F., A. Eisner, M. Gregory, & J. Ristuccia. 2013. *Helping Traumatized Children Learn 2: Creating and Advocating for Trauma-Sensitive Schools.* Report and policy agenda. Boston: Massachusetts Advocates for Children. https://traumasensitiveschools.org/wp-content/uploads/2013/11/HTCL-Vol-2-Creating-and-Advocating-for-TSS.pdf.

Fox, L., & M.L. Hemmeter. 2009. "A Program-Wide Model for Supporting Social Emotional Development and Addressing Challenging Behavior in Early Childhood Settings." *In Handbook of Positive Behavior Support,* eds. W. Sailor, G. Dunlap, G. Sugai, & R. Horner, 177–202. New York: Springer.

Ginsburg, K.R. 2007. "The Importance of Play in Promoting Healthy Child Development and Maintaining Strong Parent–Child Bonds." *Pediatrics* 119 (1): 182–91. http://pediatrics.aappublications.org/content/119/1/182.full.

Herman, J. [1992] 1997. *Trauma and Recovery: The Aftermath of Violence—From Domestic Abuse to Political Terror.* New York: Basic.

HHS (US Department of Health and Human Services, Administration on Children, Youth, and Families, Children's Bureau). 2015. *Child Maltreatment 2015.* Annual report. www.acf.hhs.gov/cb/report/child-maltreatment-2015.

Koomar, J.A. 2009. "Trauma- and Attachment-Informed Sensory Integration Assessment and Intervention." *Sensory Integration: Special Interest Section Quarterly* 32 (4): 1–4.

Koplow, L., & J. Ferber. 2007. "The Traumatized Child in Preschool." Chap. 10 in *Unsmiling Faces: How Preschools Can Heal*, 2nd ed., ed. L. Koplow, 175–93. New York: Teachers College Press.

NAEYC. 2022. *Developmentally Appropriate Practice in Early Childhood Programs Serving Children from Birth Through Age 8*. 4th ed. Washington, DC: NAEYC.

NCTSNSC (National Child Traumatic Stress Network Schools Committee). 2008. *Child Trauma Toolkit for Educators*. Los Angeles, CA, & Durham, NC: NCTSNSC. www.nctsn.org/resources/child-trauma-toolkit-educators.

Perry, B.D., & M. Szalavitz. 2006. *The Boy Who Was Raised as a Dog: And Other Stories from a Child Psychiatrist's Notebook— What Traumatized Children Can Teach Us About Loss, Love, and Healing*. New York: Basic.

Porges, S.W. 2004. "Neuroception: A Subconscious System for Detecting Threats and Safety." *ZERO TO THREE* 24 (5): 19–24.

Siegel, D.J. 2012. *The Developing Mind: How Relationships and the Brain Interact to Shape Who We Are*. 2nd ed. New York: Guilford.

Stacks, A.M., & T. Oshio. 2009. "Disorganized Attachment and Social Skills as Indicators of Head Start Children's School Readiness Skills." *Attachment and Human Development* 11 (2): 143–64.

Streeck-Fischer, A., & B.A. van der Kolk. 2000. "Down Will Come Baby, Cradle and All: Diagnostic and Therapeutic Implications of Chronic Trauma on Child Development." *Australian and New Zealand Journal of Psychiatry* 34 (6): 903–18.

Stubenbort, K., M.M. Cohen, & V. Trybalski. 2010. "The Effectiveness of an Attachment-Focused Treatment Model in a Therapeutic Preschool for Abused Children." *Clinical Social Work Journal* 38 (1): 51–60.

van der Kolk, B.A. 2003. "The Neurobiology of Childhood Trauma and Abuse." *Child and Adolescent Psychiatric Clinics* 12 (2): 293–317.

van der Kolk, B.A. 2005. "Developmental Trauma Disorder: Toward a Rational Diagnosis for Children with Complex Trauma Histories." *Psychiatric Annals* 35 (5): 401–8.

Wolpow, R., M.M. Johnson, R. Hertel, & S.O. Kincaid. 2009. *The Heart of Learning and Teaching: Compassion, Resiliency, and Academic Success*. Olympia, WA: State Office of Superintendent of Public Instruction, Compassionate Schools. www.k12.wa.us/sites/default/files/public/compassionateschools/pubdocs/theheartoflearningandteaching.pdf.

Wright, T. 2014. "Too Scared to Learn: Teaching Young Children Who Have Experienced Trauma." Research in Review. *Young Children* 69 (5): 88–93.

Reflection Questions

1. Since this article's original publication, traumatic events have likely impacted even more young children. In your experience, what are some sources of that trauma, and how have you observed their effects? See the discussion of children's anxieties, stress, and trauma on pages 113–115 in *Developmentally Appropriate Practice* (NAEYC 2022).

2. What kinds of resources and supports do you need in order to try out the ideas presented in this article? Where might you begin to find these supports in your workplace or community?

3. Think about a time when you worked with a child who was having difficulty managing or regulating their emotions. What strategies did you use to support their self-regulation? What other strategies mentioned in this article might you try? For a helpful discussion about the role of self-regulation, see page 117 in *Developmentally Appropriate Practice* (NAEYC 2022).

4. Describe how your current practices reflect the healthy, consistent interactions young trauma survivors need to support their healthy brain development. Are these practices helpful for all children, not only those who have experienced trauma? What additional practices might be beneficial for you to implement? Consider the age-specific practices described in Chapter 6 (pages 121–143) in *Developmentally Appropriate Practice* (NAEYC 2022).

5. From the article's discussion and your experience, how might trauma interfere with young children's imaginative play? How might you support the play of young children in your classroom who have experienced trauma?

6. Are there professionals (e.g., child mental health specialists, social workers, school psychologists) with whom you might talk about the issues discussed in this article? Develop a list of resources for in-person or online support on these difficult issues.

About the Author

Katie Statman-Weil, EdD, LCSW, is an educator and psychotherapist. She is also a speaker and trainer on childhood trauma, mental health, and classroom management. Katie consults with schools to create relationship-based and trauma-responsive environments to improve educational experiences for all learners. Additionally, she is a parenting therapist and coach, education consultant, and adjunct professor.

Supporting Anxious Children in the Preschool Classroom

Sierra L. Brown, Allison Aberson, Stephanie Easley, and Kara E. McGoey

Joshua, a 3-year-old in Mrs. Adams's classroom, has been anxious since the first day of preschool and continues to show anxious behaviors two months later. Joshua's challenging behaviors seem to heighten at morning drop-off, during transitions and changes in the classroom schedule, and during free play throughout the day. Mrs. Adams has observed that Joshua is often inconsolable and noncompliant: he screams, stands by the door, complains of stomachaches, and repeatedly asks when his mother will return.

In the past, Mrs. Adams has had children in her classroom who showed some sadness when their families dropped them off, but for most of those children, the sadness decreased over time. She is concerned that Joshua's behaviors have not improved with experience and time in the program. Mrs. Adams is looking for effective techniques and strategies that will reduce Joshua's anxiety—particularly techniques that are easily incorporated into the classroom routine.

Authors' Note

The coronavirus pandemic is a shared traumatic event that has directly and indirectly impacted the lives of many families across the United States and the world. For children, this unprecedented event has resulted in uncertainty and the disruption of daily life. For younger children, adapting to the "new normal" of life during coronavirus can be confusing and disorienting. Many schools and early childhood education centers across the United States have been closed, causing a disruption in child care and education. Daily routines have been changed, and it's difficult for many young children to understand why. As a result, many children may be experiencing heightened anxiety and worry. For children who are especially sensitive to anxiety, recent events may have amplified these feelings. Children have been impacted by COVID-19 in many different ways and are acutely aware of the changes in their everyday life. For some children, early childhood education programs provide a safe haven that is predictable and safe, and children now may feel disconnected from their friends and family. For other children, the transition back to their routines and to early childhood education settings may be especially difficult. As with any difficult situation, parents, teachers, and other supportive adults should explain these events and recent changes in age-appropriate and developmentally appropriate ways. Many of the strategies discussed in this article can be adapted to use with worries surrounding COVID-19 and the return-to-school routines.

Going to an early childhood education program can be a frightening experience for many young children. While most children become accustomed to the routine of going to school or to another type of early care and education program, some children continue to be anxious for some time. For preschool-age children, evidence of anxiousness in the classroom includes general distress, clinginess, excessive worry, separation fears, somatic complaints, sleep difficulties, and repetitive and perfectionistic behaviors (Mian et al. 2012). Whether observed anxiousness in the classroom is due to shyness, inhibition, or an anxiety-related disorder, teachers can be crucial in helping children adjust and cope.

Generalized anxiety, separation anxiety, and social phobias are the most commonly diagnosed disorders in early childhood, and research has suggested that up to 19 percent of young children display clinically significant symptoms of anxiety (Bufferd et al. 2012; Fox et al. 2012; Franz et al. 2013). Most children who met criteria for an anxiety disorder at age 3 continued to meet criteria at age 5 (Bufferd et al. 2012). Teachers may not initially address anxiousness because mild anxious behaviors in young children are common (Marakovitz et al. 2011). It is often difficult to differentiate between typical anxieties of early childhood and more serious concerns, as many young children may be shy or timid or may express specific fears. However, anxiety differs from common childhood fears and is determined by the behavior's severity, duration, and significant impact on a child's ability to function (Broeren et al. 2013).

Although they may not experience anxiety as severe as Joshua, all children who are anxious can benefit from interventions and activities that help them develop coping skills. Translating therapeutic techniques for use in the preschool classroom is a great way to support young children. The techniques described in the following sections are common, evidence-based strategies that mental health professionals use to teach young children emotional regulation and coping skills. These activities are essential components of evidence-based therapies such as cognitive behavioral therapy (CBT), commonly used to treat anxiety disorders. CBT techniques include modeling, affective education, self-instruction, problem solving, and relaxation training.

Educators like Mrs. Adams can implement various classroom management and play-based therapeutic techniques that target anxious symptoms in children. Even without formal training in therapeutic techniques, the techniques presented in this article are practical tips that can be easily integrated into the early childhood education setting. These techniques help guide teachers in making informed decisions about appropriate ways to respond to young children's anxiety. The strategies include classroom management techniques, de-escalation techniques, and play-based therapeutic techniques often used in play therapy for children with significant anxiety symptoms. Teachers can implement these strategies with an individual child or with a group of children in a preschool classroom.

Classroom Management Techniques

Children spend many hours during the day participating in play activities. Play helps children develop important cognitive, social, and emotional skills. It enables children to express themselves and to construct an understanding of the world while fostering problem-solving skills, social skills, and language development (Yogman et al. 2018). As a developmentally appropriate approach used to assist children in expressing themselves, play allows children to process emotional and behavioral difficulties and helps them work on coping strategies to handle future setbacks (Schaefer 2010; Schaefer & Drewes 2018).

The goal of classroom management techniques is to build on a child's skills to decrease their anxiety in the classroom and to help the child learn to cope and become more independent in the future. Important strategies for teachers to use when interacting with children who are overly anxious are (a) limiting choice, (b) providing structure through routine, and (c) using therapeutic limit setting. Here, we explain these strategies in more detail. The table "Classroom Management Techniques for Preschoolers Experiencing Anxiety" on page 80 includes some additional strategies.

Limiting Choice

Many preschool classrooms are organized in a manner that enables children to make choices and gives them opportunities to develop decision-making skills. However, this can be overwhelming for children who have significant anxiety and who experience difficulty making decisions (Goodyear-Brown 2011). Free play in particular can be disorienting for children with significant anxiety because of the reliance on unstructured and independent activities (Goodyear-Brown 2011). Behavior difficulties may appear during this unstructured time, especially for children with anxiety.

Joshua has to make many decisions during free play, such as which toys he wants to play with, whom he wants to play with, what area he should go to, and what rules to follow in that area. He may also be fearful of making the "wrong" decision. These pressures may be triggers for his anxiety and lead to Joshua showing challenging behavior or expressing anxious worries.

A teacher can help a child like Joshua and prevent some of those behaviors by limiting their choices. Limiting choices provides the structure a child who experiences anxiety needs during an otherwise unstructured time while also providing opportunities to build decision-making skills, as the activity calls for. Teachers can limit the choices in the classroom to two or three preferred activities or toys.

Limited choice is often used as a therapeutic strategy not only for reducing anxious or challenging behaviors but also for increasing children's compliance to engage in nonpreferred activities (activities children tend to avoid) and for supporting children in building their skills (Goodyear-Brown 2011). To implement limited choice, teachers can identify learning areas where there may be too many choices for an anxious child, develop a plan to structure those areas, and model decision-making skills for the child.

Limiting materials can help children make decisions and maintain organization in the classroom. For example, instead of offering all of the blocks—wooden unit blocks, LEGO bricks, brush blocks—at the same time, the teacher can reorganize the block area to include just two main types of blocks and some supporting materials. The teacher can periodically rotate the supporting toys in the block area, eventually making all the toys available over time. Not only will this limit choice and help structure block activities, it will also maintain the children's interest in that area.

Providing Structure Through Routine

In addition to structuring the classroom's physical organization, it is important for teachers to evaluate the schedule as well to identify areas in the daily routine in which to limit choices so as to benefit children who may need more structure to make decisions. As teachers know, routine and adherence to the daily schedule are important. Routine and structure are key in managing symptoms of anxiety in young children (Goodyear-Brown 2011). A classroom schedule enables children to anticipate what is going to come next, thus alleviating anxious feelings. When possible, each activity should have clear expectations and guidelines, with a specific start and end time and both a five-minute and a two-minute warning (such as ringing a bell) to alert children to the approaching end of the activity. Transitions from one activity to another are situations that can lack structure and may cause some difficulty. To reduce challenging behavior, setting clear rules and behavioral expectations for transitions and, as much as possible, minimizing time between activities will help all children, but especially children with anxiety (Hulac & Briesch 2017). Changes in the schedule may also trigger anxiety; being responsive to children with anxiety will mean giving them warnings ahead of time about any schedule changes and providing a clear plan for the next activity (Goodyear-Brown 2011).

Using Therapeutic Limit Setting

As in play therapy, therapeutic limit setting in the classroom is necessary to allow children with anxiety to express their feelings. Limit setting also provides parameters, which contribute to structure in the classroom and help ensure safety and security for all children.

Young children with anxiety often use challenging behaviors that pose safety concerns (to themselves and to others) and disrupt learning. Limits on a child's behavior serve not only to allow the child to express themselves in a positive manner but also to do so safely (Drewes & Schaefer 2018). Although some flexibility is needed between the child and the teacher (e.g., providing structured choices), disruptive, destructive, or aggressive behavior must be firmly addressed.

Limits should be applied in ways that provide a child with opportunities to take ownership of their behavior. For example, if a child begins to throw blocks, the teacher can respond in a way that acknowledges the child's feelings, provides corrective feedback, and enables the child to correct the behavior on their own. The teacher can say, "Throwing blocks can hurt other children. I can see that you are upset, but the blocks are for building, not for throwing. You can keep building with the blocks or you can go to the calm-down area to calm down." In response to the teacher's intervention, the child in this example chose to retrieve the thrown blocks and add them to their structure. In giving the child the power to choose how to deal with their big feelings, the teacher supports the child's ownership of their feelings and the appropriate ways to address them. The purpose of limit setting in the classroom is not only to provide the boundaries of acceptable behavior but also to give the child an opportunity to self-regulate.

De-Escalation Techniques for Addressing Anxiety

While the vast majority of children's challenging behaviors do not meet the criteria for a clinical diagnosis of anxiety disorder, even a low level of anxiety can significantly affect a child's ability to integrate into the classroom. At first, a child's behaviors may appear similar to noncompliance or tantrum behaviors when in fact the cause is anxiety. There are several strategies that teachers can use to support children and de-escalate their anxiety if their anxious behaviors become disruptive.

During a tantrum or a meltdown, it is difficult for children to follow any sort of directions, rules, or expectations. If a child is engaging in anxious, fearful, or tantrum behaviors, the teacher's first step is to use a soft tone of voice and provide the child with a model of calm breathing—while the teacher remains calm and avoids showing the frustration they may be experiencing (Goodyear-Brown 2011; Goodyear-Brown & Anderson 2018). The teacher can encourage deep breathing, teaching and modeling for the child how to take deep, long breaths to first slow their thinking and then calm their body.

For disruptive behavior, it is important to keep directions brief and to the point, such as, "You must keep your feet on the floor" and "You need to use an inside voice." In addition, teachers should avoid why questions ("Why did you hit Keysha?" or "Why are you so sad when Mom leaves?") during the initial de-escalation and instead focus on validating the child by saying something like, "I understand that you are upset right now." *Why* questions are often difficult for young children to answer; however, through teachers' validating statements, children have space to experience their emotions and benefit from strategies that can help them calm down. When a child has calmed, ended the tantrum, or relaxed their body through breathing, then the teacher can focus on addressing the source of their anxiety.

The teacher can find a quiet corner and ask the child to talk about the source of their anxiety or can assist the child with labeling their feelings. Start with a statement such as, "I noticed you became really upset when we ran out of time for story time." The teacher can then work with the child to identify their feelings and behaviors ("When you became angry that we ran out of time for story time, you ran and hid in the library area"), work on coping skills, and together think about appropriate behaviors to use the next time the child experiences those feelings ("What are things you can do instead of hiding to help you when you are angry?"). To prevent more behavior problems later, it is important that the child completely calms down before reengaging in classroom activities (Goodyear-Brown 2011).

The three activities that follow can be useful in targeting anxiety—two are used for de-escalating children's anxious behaviors, and the third assists children in identifying the cause of their anxiety and in developing coping skills. Teachers can teach these skill-building strategies to individual children or they can integrate them into the day's activities to share with the whole class.

Bubble Blowing

Deep breathing exercises slow the body's arousal reaction to anxiety and encourage relaxation. Bubble blowing is a deep breathing technique used in play therapy, incorporating a fun activity into teaching children a specific strategy to control breathing when they become angry or upset (Barrett et al. 2019; Goodyear-Brown 2011; Hall, Kaduson, & Schaefer 2002; Knell & Dasari 2016). This is effective for children who are inhibited by their anxiety.

To initiate the activity with the entire class, the teacher uses bubble solution and a wand to blow bubbles around the room, and the children play with the bubbles. After a couple of minutes, the teacher invites the children to each blow their own big, imaginary bubbles. The teacher first explains how to take a deep breath, then demonstrates. The teacher tells the children to fill their lungs with air and slowly blow out the air as if blowing a big bubble. The teacher reminds the children that blowing too fast or too hard will pop the bubble and will not calm their bodies.

The next step is to have the children practice blowing bubbles themselves. While children are waiting to take their turn with the bubble wand, the teacher can encourage them to continue practicing breathing by imagining they are blowing bubbles. The teacher explains that blowing bubbles when they become upset, worried, or nervous will help them calm down and control their behavior.

Classroom Management Techniques for Preschoolers Experiencing Anxiety

Time of day	Techniques
Drop-off	› Work with family members to create a routine for morning drop-off so children know what to expect. This will also make the transition from home to school easier. › Keep goodbyes warm but brief. › Provide distraction from separation from primary caregivers by preparing some highly motivating activities for children to do in the morning (such as reading a story together or doing an art project).
Circle time	› Create a visual schedule and review it daily with the children. › Check in with the children about how they are feeling. Use visual tools to explain and to help label different emotions.
Free play	› Limit the number of choices for free play, or provide a choice between limited areas (for example, "You can choose to play in the block area or in the dramatic play center"). › Pair children who are familiar with each other in order to provide comfort.
Playground	› Provide calm activities, like drawing with sidewalk chalk, reading, or blowing bubbles in addition to standard playground activities. It can be overwhelming for some children to engage in group play. › Teachers can introduce structured games and activities that children can elect to play. These games may help reduce anxiety that is caused by joining a group or uncertainty of what to play.
Throughout the day	› Let children carry comfort items, as appropriate (a favorite stuffed animal, a photo of family members). › Be consistent! Keep the daily routine as steady as possible. This could include developing consistent lesson plans for each day of the week.

Happy Space

Positive imagery can be an effective tool for helping preschoolers relax when they are anxious (Goodyear-Brown 2011). This strategy is based on the guided therapeutic imagery technique that is used in many therapeutic modalities. The primary goal of guided imagery is for the individual to create a positive image in their mind, incorporating all their senses to promote relaxation.

Because guided imagery is an imagined exercise, very young children may have difficulty doing this independently. It may be helpful to young children to offer a more concrete activity to promote relaxation, such as setting aside a physical space in the classroom where they can go to engage in positive imagery. The Happy Space can create space for a child to engage their senses and decrease anxiety. The Happy Space can be a place that contains warm, comfortable materials such as soft pillows, blankets, beanbags, and rugs. The teacher can invite the children to provide input into the design of the Happy Space, decorating it with pictures of things that the children enjoy—family members, pets or other animals, characters from cartoons or children's literature—and that encourage comfort. If children have preferred stuffed animals or blankets, this area would be a good place to allow them to use their security objects to help them self-soothe during times of anxiety.

It is important to distinguish that this space is a calming, happy space and not a space used for punishment or as a consequence for challenging behavior. The Happy Space is an area where children can go when they feel sad, anxious, or worried, signaling to the teacher that something is wrong. Having a space for children to decompress encourages more positive behavior from the children rather than behaviors such as tantrums.

Teacher-Family Collaboration

As a close daily observer of a child with anxious behaviors, a teacher should be aware of additional supports and interventions that may be available to help the child. This includes assistance from a mental health professional (e.g., behavior specialist, therapist, pediatric psychiatrist or psychologist) who may be available to support the child in the classroom. Such a professional can help early childhood education programs develop additional behavior supports or determine whether the child's behaviors suggest more serious concerns.

When identifying whether a child might benefit from additional help, the teacher should collaborate with the child's family. An open discussion regarding the teacher's concerns about the child's anxiety should occur with the family. Collaboration with primary caregivers offers teachers insight into whether the challenging behaviors happen in contexts other than school, the severity of the behaviors, and effective strategies used at home. Collaboration also offers the family opportunities to gain important information about their child's functioning in the classroom. Additional behaviors that indicate a child may benefit from professional help are whether the child avoids certain places or reacts to situations in ways that seem disproportionate to the events.

If it is determined that additional supports may be needed to assist the child in the classroom, teachers should consult with their supervisor or administration regarding the process to obtain these supportive services in the classroom. Additional assistance from a mental health or behavioral health professional can be very useful when the child's anxiety is impacting their success in the classroom. The team can work collaboratively to determine if additional help is needed in the classroom with behavioral health professionals or outside of the school context.

Additionally, a referral for early childhood services through special education may be appropriate. Typically, there are procedures established by the early childhood program on how to obtain this assistance, and these procedures are based on the laws and regulations proposed by the Individuals with Disabilities Education Act (2004). These procedures outline action steps necessary in the identification, diagnosis, and services that can be provided to a young child through special education services. Early childhood programs can reach out to their early intervention service agency or local mental health agencies for needed support.

When a child is in the Happy Space, the teacher should always use positive strategies, prompting the child to reflect back and problem solve by recognizing and talking about their upsetting feelings and thinking about positive behaviors they could use whenever those feelings surface. The teacher may want to create a social story to guide the child in decompressing or supply picture books that encourage strategies.

A young child may need guidance and scaffolding from an adult to use imagery while in the Happy Space. Over time, with practice when both calm and upset, the child will begin to use the skills on their own.

Worry Can

The Worry Can strategy helps children identify their worries and develop appropriate coping skills (Goodyear-Brown & Anderson 2018). The teacher can facilitate discussion and problem solving of worries and anxiety through this activity. The teacher and the child experiencing anxiety work together to decorate the child's own Worry Can—a can that has a reclosable lid or a removable top with a slit in it. The teacher then encourages the child to draw their worries on pieces of paper and supports the child by writing the specific worries under the drawings. The child then puts their drawings inside the can. This activity allows the child to express their fears instead of keeping them bottled up, which can exacerbate the symptoms of anxiety.

To implement the Worry Can activity, Mrs. Adams introduces it to Joshua and invites him to decorate the can with her. Mrs. Adams then asks Joshua how he feels when he is worried or anxious and to identify some circumstances in which he feels anxious. This ensures that Joshua has some understanding of his own feelings and behaviors.

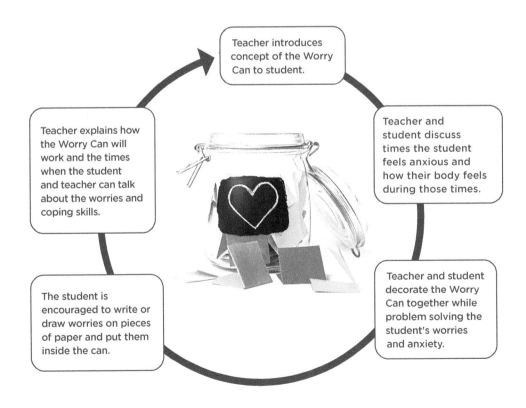

Teacher introduces concept of the Worry Can to student.

Teacher and student discuss times the student feels anxious and how their body feels during those times.

Teacher and student decorate the Worry Can together while problem solving the student's worries and anxiety.

The student is encouraged to write or draw worries on pieces of paper and put them inside the can.

Teacher explains how the Worry Can will work and the times when the student and teacher can talk about the worries and coping skills.

Once Mrs. Adams and Joshua have talked about things that make him anxious, she explains to him how the Worry Can works. Mrs. Adams tells Joshua that the Worry Can is a special place where he can put his worries after drawing them and, together, writing them down. She explains that the worries go into the can so they do not keep bothering him while he is having fun. During special times three mornings a week, Mrs. Adams and Joshua will read the worries together and talk about them, along with ways to deal with his scary feelings. Over time, the expectation is that Joshua will become more independent and will use the Worry Can without Mrs. Adams, drawing or "writing" about his worries himself and dropping them in the can.

However, even when Joshua uses the Worry Can independently, Mrs. Adams knows it is important to be consistent in working with him and in using their designated times together to help him develop and practice the crucial coping skills that are necessary to alleviate some of his anxieties.

Conclusion

Many preschoolers exhibit anxious behaviors: controlling behaviors, tantrums, crying, and somatic complaints are common symptoms of anxiety. Preschool teachers are crucial in promoting children's acquisition of cognitive and academic skills, and they are equally important in helping young children develop social and emotional skills. With a repertory of strategies for relieving anxiety, teachers can help all young children develop the coping skills they need to deal with stressors in the classroom.

The techniques described here have been shown to be effective in individual therapy, in group therapy, and as classroom interventions, and they are used in many different treatment modalities. Many curricula targeting young children's social and emotional development employ similar strategies to foster affective regulation and coping skills as part of the intervention.

Reflection Questions

1. How may the article's insights, as well as discussion of children's anxieties, stress, and trauma on pages 113–115 in *Developmentally Appropriate Practice* (NAEYC 2022), help you in your efforts to support the children in your program? Are there particular children you think would especially benefit from the approaches described in this article? Reread the article with one or more of those children in mind.

2. The article includes a note about COVID-19 and its potential impact on young children's anxiety. Talk with a colleague or other partner about those impacts, how you have seen them manifest, and how you might help children and families through this anxious time.

3. The article describes several kinds of therapeutic techniques that can be adapted to an early learning setting. Choose at least one of these techniques, make a plan to implement it, and observe and document its effects.

4. Early childhood practices like the use of flexible schedules and unstructured free play may be overwhelming for some children with anxiety. In these situations, what is developmentally appropriate? As you reflect on potentially effective practices that are developmentally appropriate, refer to the core considerations of individuality and context on pages 20–22 in *Developmentally Appropriate Practice* (NAEYC 2022).

5. How do the discussions of setting limits fit with your own teaching experiences? What have been your successes and challenges in addressing anxiety and challenging behavior through limit setting to help children stay safe and secure? The discussion of positive behavior on pages 117–119 in *Developmentally Appropriate Practice* (NAEYC 2022) offers a helpful context.

6. If appropriate for the ages and developmental characteristics of the children you teach, try out one of the three de-escalation techniques described in this article and document the effects. Do you have other, similar techniques that you have found helpful?

Just like learning the alphabet, children need repeated and consistent teaching and practice for strategies to be effective in managing anxious symptoms. It is important for teachers and families to communicate closely about successful strategies—strategies both at school and at home—so they can use them consistently in both contexts. (See "Teacher-Family Collaboration" on page 81.)

Young children benefit from recognizing their strong emotions and from learning that they can control them. With time and practice, teachers may see improvement in a child's ability to initiate coping mechanisms or in a child's initiative to request help from an adult in handling their strong emotions. As every child is different, improvement might be observed immediately or over several months. However, any small improvement or skill gained can greatly increase a child's ability to participate, learn, and engage with others in the classroom.

REFERENCES

Barrett, P., N. Games, B. Fisak, P. Stallard, & L. Phillips. 2019. "The Treatment of Anxiety Disorders in Preschool-Aged Children." In *Anxiety in Preschool Children: Assessment, Treatment, and Prevention,* eds. B. Fisak & P. Barrett, 114–41. New York: Routledge.

Broeren, S., P. Muris, S. Diamantopoulou, & J.R. Baker. 2013. "The Course of Childhood Anxiety Symptoms: Developmental Trajectories and Child-Related Factors in Normal Children." *Journal of Abnormal Child Psychology* 41 (1): 81–95.

Bufferd, S.J., L.R. Dougherty, G.A. Carlson, S. Rose, & D.N. Klein. 2012. "Psychiatric Disorders in Preschoolers: Continuity from Ages 3 to 6." *The American Journal of Psychiatry* 169 (11): 1157–64.

Drewes, A.A., & C.E. Schaefer, eds. 2018. *Play-Based Interventions for Childhood Anxieties, Fears, and Phobias.* New York: Guilford.

Fox, J.K., C.M. Warner, A.B. Lerner, K. Ludwig, J.L. Ryan, D. Colognori, C.P. Lucas, & L.M. Brotman. 2012. "Preventive Intervention for Anxious Preschoolers and Their Parents: Strengthening Early Emotional Development." *Child Psychiatry & Human Development* 43 (4): 544–59.

Franz, L., A. Angold, W. Copeland, E.J. Costello, N. Towe- Goodman, & H. Egger. 2013. "Preschool Anxiety Disorders in Pediatric Primary Care: Prevalence and Comorbidity." *Journal of the American Academy of Child & Adolescent Psychiatry* 52 (12): 1294–303.

Goodyear-Brown, P. 2011. "The Worry Wars: A Protocol for Treating Childhood Anxiety Disorders." In *Integrative Play Therapy,* eds. A.A. Drewes, S.C. Bratton, & C.E. Schaefer, 129–51. Hoboken, NJ: John Wiley & Sons.

Goodyear-Brown, P., & E. Andersen. 2018. "Play Therapy for Separation Anxiety in Children." In *Play-Based Interventions for Childhood Anxieties, Fears, and Phobias,* eds. A.A. Drewes & C.E. Schaefer, 158–76. New York: Guilford.

Hall, T.M., H.G. Kaduson, & C.E. Schaefer. 2002. "Fifteen Effective Play Therapy Techniques." *Professional Psychology: Research and Practice* 33 (6): 515–22.

Hulac, D.M., & A.M. Briesch. 2017. *Evidence-Based Strategies for Effective Classroom Management.* New York: Guilford.

Individuals with Disabilities Education Act. 2004. 20 U.S.C. § 1400.

Knell, S.M., & M. Dasari. 2016. "Cognitive-Behavioral Play Therapy for Anxiety and Depression." In *Empirically Based Play Interventions for Children,* eds. L.A. Reddy, T.M. Files-Hall, & C.E. Schaefer, 77–94. Washington, DC: American Psychological Association.

Marakovitz, S.E., R.L, Wagmiller, N.D. Mian, M.J. Briggs-Gowan, & A.S. Carter. 2011. "Lost Toy? Monsters Under the Bed? Contributions of Temperament and Family Factors to Early Internalizing Problems in Boys and Girls." *Journal of Clinical Child and Adolescent* Psychology 40 (2): 233–44.

Mian, N.D., L. Godoy, M.J. Briggs-Gowan, & A.S. Carter. 2012. "Patterns of Anxiety Symptoms in Toddlers and Preschool-Age Children: Evidence of Early Differentiation." *Journal of Anxiety Disorders* 26 (1): 102–10.

NAEYC. 2022. *Developmentally Appropriate Practice in Early Childhood Programs Serving Children from Birth Through Age 8.* 4th ed. Washington, DC: NAEYC.

Schaefer, C.E., ed. 2010. *Play Therapy for Preschool Children.* Washington, DC: American Psychological Association.

Schaefer, C.E., & A.A. Drewes. 2018. "Play-Based Approaches for Treating Childhood Anxieties: Basic Concepts and Practices." In *Play-Based Interventions for Childhood Anxieties, Fears, and Phobias,* eds. A.A. Drewes & C.E. Schaefer, 3–12. New York: Guilford.

Yogman, M., A. Garner, J. Hutchinson, K. Hirsh-Pasek, R.M. Golinkoff, the Committee on Psychosocial Aspects of Child and Family Health, & the Council on Communications and Media. 2018. "The Power of Play: A Pediatric Role in Enhancing Development in Young Children." *Pediatrics* 142 (3). https://pediatrics.aappublications.org/content/142/3/e20182058.

About the Authors

Sierra L. Brown, PhD, NCSP, ABPP, is a licensed psychologist at Milton Hershey School. Her research interests include the understanding of the social and emotional development of children diagnosed with autism spectrum disorder.

Allison Aberson, PhD, is a licensed psychologist in the state of Pennsylvania practicing at Cognitive Behavior Institute. Her research interests include preschool mental health and the impact of parental stress on behaviors throughout childhood.

Stephanie Easley, PhD, is a certified school psychologist employed by North Allegheny School District, a large suburban district in the Pittsburgh area. Stephanie has been trained to serve students in grades pre-K to 12+.

Kara E. McGoey, PhD, is a professor of school psychology at Duquesne University. Her research interests include preschool mental health and translating scientifically sound interventions into the classroom to improve students' social and emotional functioning.

Welcoming Refugee Children into Early Childhood Classrooms

Sadia Warsi

In Mr. Allen's pre-K class, the children greet their classmates in each other's home language. Seth turns to Maryam and greets her in Arabic, "Assalamu Aliakum." Maryam very softly says back, "Hello," in English. In Spanish, Tarek says, "Buenos días," and Isabella responds, "Günaydın," in Turkish.

Refugee families are a part of many communities, and they bring rich cultural experiences to early learning programs. Because of the social and emotional impact that being a refugee has on young children and their families, it is important that early childhood educators create inclusive and nurturing classroom environments.

Most children who are refugees have experienced hardship and trauma, so it's vital that they feel welcomed by teachers and peers in their new classrooms. Here are some ideas to get you started.

Prepare to Greet the Children

Work with the class to be ready to greet their new classmate in a warm and cheerful manner and to show appreciation for the child's culture. The children can learn the new child's name and how to say a few words in his or her language. They can create welcome cards and pictures for their new classmate.

Create Play Experiences that Do Not Require English

All children need opportunities to play in the classroom. If new arrivals do not speak English, it will take them some time to learn the language. In the meantime, ensure that there are games and activities available that don't require much language. Offer board games and art experiences that need little instruction (simple games, such as Candyland, and open-ended art materials). Plan activities in which children engage in creative and imaginative play using music and movement.

Here are some play-based activities for dual language learners:

> Photograph all the children in the classroom. Make a copy of each photo, and play a matching game. Write the children's names at the bottom of their photos to help them recognize their own and each other's names.

> Children can create their own musical instruments and form bands. Make maracas by filling plastic bottles with beans, create string instruments by wrapping large rubber bands around open shoe boxes, and use a comb and tissue paper to make a kazoo. Children can compose music together and invite their families to a gig.

Play-based activities help create an environment where children can work together without the need for frequent teacher mediation. This environment offers opportunities for children to connect and helps new classmates adjust to the classroom.

Familiarize Families with Classrooms

Many families—whether refugees or immigrants—come from countries where school experiences are very different from those in the United States. All families want to be involved and support their children in their new school. But sometimes it's hard for families with little or no prior school experience within early childhood settings to understand how to begin. And it can be especially confusing for families from different cultural backgrounds or who speak another language. Consider using visuals to introduce culturally and linguistically diverse families to the school environment. (See "A Picture's Worth a Thousand Words" on page 88.)

A Picture's Worth a Thousand Words

> Create a visual schedule of daily activities to help children and families understand what happens in a typical day in your classroom. Use photographs of circle time, read alouds, snack time, center time, and so on. Or you can print out pictures from the internet or cut out pictures from magazines.

> Discuss healthy eating and classroom routines and rules, such as hand washing before eating to keep everyone healthy. Use visuals with photographs. Or make short videos of routines such as snack time—children setting up the food, serving themselves, and clearing eating areas when they've finished.

> Use visuals to explain rules about expectations for classroom behavior, such as lining up for transitions, sitting on individual carpet squares, and putting away blocks in the block area.

If an interpreter is available or you can communicate verbally, talk with the parents and other caregivers about what to expect. Explain classroom routines, such as arrival and departure and the daily schedule. Talk about classroom rules. Many children who are refugees have spent unstructured time in camps or other transitional settings. Help them become part of the structured classroom routine as soon as possible.

Once they spend time in the classroom and observe their children's daily activities, families will feel more at ease and will be able to reinforce those routines at home. Inviting families and caregivers into the classroom helps build home-school relationships and encourages them to be active partners in their children's education.

Connect with Related Community Cultural Groups

Many children and teachers may not have interacted with diverse cultural groups from other countries—and particularly from countries suffering through war, famine, and other crises. It's difficult to understand the experiences of children who are refugees without first understanding their home cultures. And it also helps to be aware that there are different cultural groups within every country. One resource may be individuals who work closely with refugee families in the United States. They can offer information about particular cultures and help teachers better understand the experiences of children who are refugees.

Families who have escaped horrific conditions are not always comfortable talking about political situations in their home countries. Refugee families are trying to create a new sense of peace and calm in the lives of their children. They want to preserve their children's childhood and create new memories and positive beginnings.

Meeting Emotional Needs

Many families and preschools try to shield children from harmful images and experiences so as not to overburden them emotionally. However, children who have lived in war zones and other fraught settings have experienced trauma beyond their years and may become overwhelmed and emotionally vulnerable in certain situations.

Resources to Help Teachers Welcome Refugee Children and Families

There are a number of resources that teachers can use to learn about the refugee crisis in general as well as strategies to use in the classroom. The ones listed below are a starting point in understanding the needs of families who are refugees.

Childhood Education International https://ceinternational1892.org

"Collaborating with Refugee Resettlement Organizations: Providing a Head Start to Young Refugees," by Lyn Morland and Tarima Levine. *Young Children,* September 2016, pp. 69–75.

"How to Support Refugee Students in the ELL Classroom," by Kristina Robertson and Lydia Breiseth. Colorín Colorado www.colorincolorado.org/article/how-support-refugee-students-ell-classroom

***Raising Young Children in a New Country: Supporting Early Learning and Healthy Development.* National Center on Cultural and Linguistic Responsiveness and by Bridging Refugee Youth and Children's Services** https://eclkc.ohs.acf.hhs.gov/sites/default/files/pdf/raising-young-children-new-country.pdf

"Teaching Refugees with Limited Formal Schooling: Classroom Supports." Calgary Board of Education, Government of Alberta, Canada www.teachingrefugees.com/socio-emotional-supports/classroom-strategies

With preschoolers, typical conflicts arise while sharing materials or taking turns. They may use inappropriate language when trying to resolve these conflicts. It should come as no surprise that children who have experienced trauma may have an extra-difficult time working through common classroom conflicts. It's important to guide them in successful problem solving so they learn that they will not be punished when they make a mistake or have an outburst. It also helps all children if there is a quiet space to go to calm down, like the classroom library beanbag chair.

Reflection Questions

1. Since this article was originally published, many early learning programs have welcomed increased numbers of refugee children and families. If you have had this experience, share with a colleague or other partner.

2. Do you have family members or friends who have been refugees? If so, and if they are comfortable doing so, talk with them about their memories of that experience and use these conversations in your reflections about the role of teachers in supporting refugee children and their families.

3. Developmentally appropriate practice emphasizes affirming all children and families—their cultures, funds of knowledge, and strengths. Refer to pages 54–59 in *Developmentally Appropriate Practice* (NAEYC 2022) for an in-depth discussion on this topic. With this perspective in mind, consider what refugee children and their families bring to your early learning setting and how you may celebrate them.

4. If there are refugee families in your area, compile a list of resources for families, such as cultural groups in the community, faith communities, and sources of practical and emotional support. How might such resources also help you as a professional?

5. The article author emphasizes the value of spending one-on-one time with children who are refugees. With a colleague or other partner, think about practical strategies for how you or other teachers might manage this (e.g., modifying your schedule, getting additional help from volunteers or others, making it easier for other children to play independently). The discussion of various learning formats on pages 187–188 in *Developmentally Appropriate Practice* (NAEYC 2022), especially the intentional use of small groups, may help you identify strategies to make time for more focused interactions.

6. You may not currently teach any children who are refugees. That said, many of the recommendations in this article may be implemented to support other children with unique needs for emotional support. Refer to the discussion of children's anxieties, stress, and trauma on pages 113–115 in *Developmentally Appropriate Practice* (NAEYC 2022).

Establish One-on-One Time with Children Who Are Refugees

It's not uncommon for young children to feel lost in the classroom and to miss their families. This can be exceptionally hard for children who are refugees, because they tend to have strong attachments to their families and may have shared traumatic experiences together. One of the biggest fears many children have is losing their parents—and some may actually have lost a parent or a loved one. A few times a day, reassure children that they are safe and that their parents or caregivers will return at the end of the day. Establishing trust and maintaining a strong bond with them is key to settling refugee children in your classroom. Build with blocks or draw together during centers time. You don't need to talk much if language is a barrier.

Create Opportunities for Refugee Families to Share Their Traditions

As refugee families adjust to school and their children become comfortable with their peers, you might invite the parents or caregivers to share some of their traditions, such as celebrations, music, food, native clothing, and folktales. Offer activities like creating ornaments or other arts and crafts from their home countries. Support families by gathering materials in advance, making sure that participating doesn't cause a financial burden. Celebrate all the different cultures represented in the classroom so refugee families don't feel singled out.

Conclusion

You will find that refugee families are grateful and appreciate your support. They are eager to cooperate and collaborate to ensure that their children fit into the classroom and maintain their connections to their rich cultures.

REFERENCE

NAEYC. 2022. *Developmentally Appropriate Practice in Early Childhood Programs Serving Children from Birth Through Age 8*. 4th ed. Washington, DC: NAEYC.

About the Author

Sadia Warsi, PhD, is associate professor of special education and early childhood education at National Louis University in Chicago.

Using Nature Contact to Support Children Under Stress

Becky L. DelVecchio, Susan Ferguson, and Wesley Knapp

All children experience stress at one time or another, and there are people, strategies, and systems in place to guide them through stressful situations and emotions. As adults working in the field of early childhood education, we have the responsibility to help children develop positive ways to manage a variety of emotions, including stress. To do so, we can think both widely and creatively to tap into and share tools and resources, including in nature.

Contact with nature can help mitigate the negative effects of stress and can help boost resilience across one's lifespan. Through nature-based encounters, we can provide children with strategies to use while they are in our care and beyond. Indeed, by using readily available natural materials or environments, these techniques have the added benefit of being accessible indoors or out, at home or away, and within or outside of early learning programs.

In this article, we share several scenarios depicting children experiencing stress in two different classroom settings. After each one, we describe nature-based strategies that an early childhood educator used to offer support and encourage resilience in those children.

Stressful Situations and Nature-Based Supports

> Three-year-old Lenny wants to play with Sandeep. He chooses a spot to play near Sandeep, looks over at him several times, and offers toys to Sandeep three times. Sandeep does not return any of Lenny's social overtures. When asked by his teacher, Mr. Ortega, if he wants to play with Lenny, Sandeep shouts *no*. When Lenny hears this, he becomes increasingly anxious and desperate for the attention of his classmate and begins to shout loudly, "No! No! No!"

Lenny was trying, unsuccessfully, to connect with another child. Although each of his and Sandeep's behaviors were appropriate given the situation, Lenny experienced stress. Lenny became overwhelmed with his "big" emotions and needed the support of his teacher to help him cope with them. To support Lenny, Mr. Ortega took several steps, including incorporating natural objects into the support he offered.

First, Mr. Ortega offered Lenny the responsibility of a "very important classroom job." That job was to feed the class pet, a fish, and to check that the water pump was still running. They also observed the aquatic plants that were anchored underneath the rocks, which grew upward and swayed with the movement of the water. Then, Lenny and Mr. Ortega used the class camera to take as many photos of the fish as Lenny liked. Later, he chose one to print.

Throughout, Mr. Ortega was careful to encourage Lenny's independence while giving him the time and space he needed to feel better. For example, Mr. Ortega verbally described Lenny's feelings and actions, so he could begin to do the same. He said "Lenny, you are upset. You were yelling when Sandeep did not want to play with you. That must have felt very hard to hear. I can help you find a way to feel better. I remember that you like the fish. Would you like to come take pictures with the camera for our art wall?" This allowed Lenny the opportunity to begin to normalize his upset feelings, to know that they are okay to have, and to understand that he could find another way to express them and start to feel better.

Ultimately, feeding, observing, and photographing the class fish helped Lenny to focus on something other than the attention he was not receiving from his classmate. It redirected his energy to another task, and it helped mitigate his feelings of disappointment or anxiety by fostering his sense of independence. Over time, and with similar supports, Lenny will be able to redirect his energy more efficiently when he is feeling stressed.

Four-year-old Fabiola misses her family when she is at school. She stays near her teacher, Ms. Paul; her voice shakes; and she is often close to tears. She does not play. Instead, she primarily watches the other children play and engage in activities as she clings to Ms. Paul.

Fabiola was struggling with separating from her family and the feelings of missing them throughout the day. Ms. Paul noticed that when she became involved in a specific task, especially one with concrete objects, Fabiola demonstrated fewer anxious emotions and behaviors. Ms. Paul started to plan nature-based activities to offer Fabiola upon her arrival each morning.

For example, Ms. Paul began with a nature-based scavenger hunt for Fabiola to complete. The scavenger hunt included items that Fabiola could find on the playground or around the school building. Fabiola then presented the items to her family at pick-up time. Ms. Paul made sure to include a variety of natural objects with different characteristics: some were soft plants like lambs-ears and pussy willows; some were spiky like pinecones, burdocks, and cacti; some were aromatic like roses, mint, and lavender; and some even liked to hide in cracks like mosses and lichens. Several days after Ms. Paul implemented this technique, she noticed Fabiola making scavenger hunts for other children.

Fabiola's introduction to natural materials and her ensuing fascination with finding them helped to reduce her stress and to demonstrate resilience. She took on a leadership role in the classroom while sharing one of her passions with other children. Building these positive connections with others, through her own nature connection, aided Fabiola in feeling more in control of herself and her environment.

Five-year-old Maya becomes angry several times a day while attending her early learning program. For example, over the past year, if her parents do not pack her favorite face mask, she refuses to wear one altogether. This causes her to have to play in one-person spots because her school requires social distancing when children do not wear masks, which frustrates Maya further.

Maya's teacher, Mr. Ortega, noticed that several children needed mask breaks throughout the day. Wearing masks has been challenging for some children, and the requirement to wear them has caused stress for both children and teachers. To alleviate the isolation of the one-person play spots, Mr. Ortega created a classroom garden just outside the class door, where mask breaks were allowed. Although the area outside the school was mostly paved, the teacher brought in large pots and potting soil for children to use for gardening. Mr. Ortega planned several adult-directed planting activities that ensured the plants would grow, but Maya's favorite part of outdoor gardening was the independent garden pots. There, children planted and nurtured whatever they liked in their own pots. Just last week, Maya planted morning glories and sunflowers, which have grown quickly. Maya's frustration and anger eased because she had a task that helped her redirect her focus and feel more independent while connecting with nature, a pastime that she could access at home, at school, and in most other environments.

Outside on the playground, 4-year-old Rosalie struggles with body coordination during play. She slides down the large slide headfirst, bumping into other children who are near her. The other children decide to leave their play with Rosalie and play somewhere else. This is not the first time; Rosalie often crashes her scooter into the shed and fence as she rides. Other children try to play with her, but when she starts to get "too crashy," they seek other activities without her. Rosalie expresses stress and hurt feelings when they do.

Rosalie loved to climb. Although the trees around them were not conducive to safe climbing, Ms. Paul recommended that she try to "grip and hold" a tree in their playground area. In this activity, Rosalie put her arms around a large tree, like a hug. Then she (magically!) lifted her feet off the ground. The other children were impressed and wanted to try too. Rosalie found an activity that helped her feel more in control of her body, that was easily accessible, and that other children could do with her. This helped Rosalie feel more accepting of her own abilities and acknowledge the limits set for her at school.

Reflection Questions

1. As a child, what were your experiences in nature? Share memories with a colleague or other partner, considering the emotional impact that contact with nature may have had in your life.

2. As the article authors note, developmentally appropriate practice emphasizes the need to identify and build on children's strengths. In a caring, equitable community of learners, "each member of the community is valued by the others and is recognized for the strengths they bring" (NAEYC 2022, xxxviii). Consider the strengths of the children in your program and how nature engagement might be especially helpful to one or more of those children.

3. Consider how you might adapt one of the nature-based activities described in this article to meet the social and emotional needs of the children with whom you work. Review the examples of teaching strategies discussed on pages 183–185 in *Developmentally Appropriate Practice* (NAEYC 2022) for possible application to your nature-based activities.

4. What are the major sources of stress in the lives of the young children you know? How might nature contact help during these stressful times?

5. Even in urban settings, nature-focused experiences may be found. With a colleague or partner, explore your immediate environment and consider ways to connect the children you teach with the natural world.

6. Engagement with nature creates opportunities to link social and emotional development with multiple content areas—language, science, creative expression, and more. For key ideas about teaching content through playful whole child, experiences, see page 66–68 of *Developmentally Appropriate Practice* (NAEYC 2022).

Conclusion

NAEYC's 2020 position statement on developmentally appropriate practice states, "Early childhood educators . . . support *all* children's learning by recognizing each child as a unique individual with assets and strengths to contribute to the early childhood education learning environment." Teachers can use nature contact to connect each child's strengths to build their recognition and regulation of the stressful feelings they may experience in a moment and over time. These stress management strategies do not require special materials that can only be found in the classroom. Rather, they make use of natural materials that children can access in most environments. This is a critical feature of helping children develop coping strategies that can be internalized and accessed throughout their lives, no matter the environments and situations in which they find themselves.

REFERENCE

NAEYC. 2022. *Developmentally Appropriate Practice in Early Childhood Programs Serving Children from Birth Through Age 8*. 4th ed. Washington, DC: NAEYC.

About the Authors

Becky L. DelVecchio, PhD, is a longtime early childhood educator, researcher, and adjunct faculty member.

Susan Ferguson, MEd, PMC, is a preschool teacher at the Wellesley College Child Study Center in Wellesley, Massachusetts.

Wesley Knapp, MS, is chief botanist at NatureServe, a conservation nonprofit based in Arlington, Virginia.

Integrating Social and Emotional Perspectives into the Curriculum

"Principle 2 [of developmentally appropriate practice] and the knowledge base that supports it strongly emphasize the importance of a curriculum that addresses academic learning along with children's social and emotional learning, development of executive function, physical movement, and play" (NAEYC 2022, 30). Educators need guidance on how to address more than one developmental domain in their teaching and how to integrate social and emotional learning into their curriculum planning for subject areas such as math, literacy, and social studies. Learning occurs across domains of child development and "each domain both supports and is supported by the others" (NAEYC 2020, 9). Social and emotional development takes a natural, central place in curriculum, whether through informal integration or intentionally planned interdisciplinary learning experiences. The benefits go both ways: children's positive emotions and interest in collaborative projects can motivate subject-area mastery, and positive experiences while learning challenging subject-area content can fuel feelings of self-esteem and pride in collective accomplishments.

The three articles in this part demonstrate how teachers can address social and emotional issues while also promoting subject-area knowledge within a caring, equitable community.

Linda M. Platas's article, "Three for One: Supporting Social, Emotional, and Mathematical Development in Preschool and Kindergarten," shows how these domains and subject areas can connect with and support one another. Teachers' mathematically supportive talk can encourage children's emotional engagement, and children's persistence and self-regulation grow when they experience meaningful, concrete, and collaborative math activities.

"Partnering with Families: Supporting Social and Emotional Development Through Picture Books," by **Alison Hooper,** suggests ways to encourage families to read with their children, not only to build literacy but also to strengthen bonds and explore emotionally and socially meaningful topics, such as bullying, self-identity, and feelings.

In "Paired Learning: Strategies for Enhancing Social Competence in Dual Language Classrooms," **Iliana Alanís** and **María Guadalupe Arreguín** describe the value of paired learning activities for both subject-area knowledge and social and emotional development. The strategies the authors highlight show how teachers can help all children, including dual language learners, develop the social skills needed to work enjoyably with a partner.

REFERENCES

NAEYC. 2020. "Developmentally Appropriate Practice." Position statement. Washington, DC: NAEYC. www.naeyc.org/resources/position-statements/dap.

NAEYC. 2022. *Developmentally Appropriate Practice in Early Childhood Programs Serving Children from Birth Through Age 8.* 4th ed. Washington, DC: NAEYC.

Three for One

Supporting Social, Emotional, and Mathematical Development in Preschool and Kindergarten

Linda M. Platas

In the back corner of Ms. Jamil's preschool classroom, Callie, Niraj, Micah, and Tracy are playing Chutes and Ladders while two of their friends look on. The players take turns, spinning the arrow and advancing their markers on the board. When Tracy's spin results in her marker climbing a ladder to a higher row of numbers, the onlookers cheer quietly, exclaiming, "Score!" When Niraj's spin results in a slide down a chute to a row of lower numbers, they sympathetically cry out, "Oh, no!"

In another area of the classroom, Lila, Iris, and Jasmine play with dominoes, matching the tiles end-to-end to create as long a row of dominoes as they can. When no further matches are possible, with Ms. Jamil's help, the girls count the number of tiles they used and write the total on a chart that lists the tallies from previous games. Iris, Lila, and Jasmine check to see how their current row, stretching from one side of the carpet to the other, compares with previous efforts.

What do these scenes have in common? They depict math activities that support the development of social and emotional skills. While children are learning about counting, quantity, and data analysis, they are also taking turns, encouraging one another, and working collaboratively. Many teachers feel pressure to prepare children for more rigorous academic challenges while simultaneously supporting their social and emotional development; it's a relief to know that these two domains can be mutually supportive.

The Mathematical Lens on Social and Emotional Development

Ensuring children's healthy social and emotional development is a primary focus for early childhood educators. Among the many skills that teachers help children develop, some of the most important are self-regulation, emotional awareness, initiative, and positive interactions (Jackson 2012). These competencies are related to positive short- and long-term outcomes, including higher academic achievement, increased well-being, and fewer conduct problems (Jones & Bouffard 2012).

Like support of social and emotional development, support of mathematical development is also crucial in early childhood classrooms (IOM & NRC 2015; NAEYC & NCTM 2010). To foster early mathematical development in young children, teachers need to understand how this development occurs—including the contribution of children's prior knowledge—and become fluent in the classroom pedagogies that support such development (Copley 2014; Sarama & Clements 2009; Zaslow 2014).

During preschool and kindergarten, children's mathematical development is promoted through engagement in a variety of activities, such as counting, comparing and contrasting quantities and shapes, performing operations, sorting and classifying, measuring, and using spatial reasoning. Children bring considerable informal mathematical understanding to the classroom; it is our job as early childhood educators to build on this informal knowledge through mathematically supportive environments, activities, and talk, as explained in the following sections.

Mathematically Supportive Environments

Classrooms that foster children's mathematical development have engaging physical features, such as student-created number walls (similar to letter walls, except with numerals and sets of objects or pictures), a variety of mathematical tools (like balance scales), manipulatives, jigsaw and geometric puzzles, blocks, pattern and shape activities, games with dice and spinners, books that promote number sense, and pretend play areas that include numerically rich materials. In the early years, hands-on interactive activities promote children's budding understanding of number, geometry, classification, and measurement.

Engaging environments such as these support lots of independence and interaction among students, which in turn foster the development of self-regulation, social awareness, and initiative. When children participate in activities based on their interests, they often show more sustained engagement and positive interactions with other children. Because they want to continue this engagement, children try to self-regulate their interactions with both the materials and the other children (Robson 2016). The more mathematically rich the classroom environment (both inside and outside), the more likely children are to find activities that spark their interest, encouraging them to draw on their mathematical knowledge along with their social and emotional skills.

Mathematically Supportive Talk

While a mathematically rich environment is important, it is only part of the equation. The quality and quantity of teachers' mathematical talk also significantly influences the growth of children's mathematical knowledge (Frye et al. 2013; Presser et al. 2015). Math talk is interactive and includes teachers talking to children, children talking to teachers, and children talking to each other. Teacher math talk incorporates vocabulary that enables us to describe our world mathematically—words and phrases like *more, less, how many, sides, angles,* and *take away*—as well as the counting numbers (*one, two, three* . . .) and the names of two- and three-dimensional shapes. (See "Mathematical Vocabulary" on page 101 for a list of key vocabulary words appropriate for early childhood classrooms.)

Mathematical Vocabulary

above	group	on top of
altogether	heavier	pattern
angle	height	plus one
backward	how many	predict
behind	in	put together
below	in front of	same
beside	in order	shape
between	just after	shorter
bottom	just before	side
check	larger	smaller
count	length	sort
count by	less than	take apart
different	long	take away
equal	longer	taller
estimate	match	top
fewer	more than	total
graph	next to	under
greater than	number	zero

As children hear math vocabulary used in context, they develop the ability to use and understand it in conversations with teachers and peers. Teachers can use math vocabulary in queries to prompt children's deeper thinking about mathematics. Open-ended questions and comments, like "How did you know how many there were?" and "Tell me how you solved that problem," encourage children to think about the mathematical process as well as verbally express their understanding. (See "Questions and Comments that Support Mathematical Thinking" on page 102 for some examples.)

In addition to explicitly supporting children's mathematical knowledge and skill acquisition, these classroom interactions require social awareness and self-regulation. These are developed through conversation turn taking, raising your hand when part of a group, and children's explanatory talk

Questions and Comments that Support Mathematical Thinking

> Tell me what is different/the same.

> How could you use a _____ to solve this problem?

> How did you figure that out?

> How did you know how many there were?

> How did you solve this problem?

> How do you know that?

> How do you know that is a triangle/square/rhombus?

> Show me how you figured that out.

> Tell me more about this problem.

> What could we use to _____?

> What do you know about the number _____?

> What do you know about _____?

> What do you notice about _____?

> What do you think comes next?

> What else do you know about _____?

> What is the pattern?

> What would happen if _____?

(NRC 2009). As children acquire math concepts and vocabulary, they also begin incorporating them into their play, which furthers their social and emotional development. For example, as children learn about time and quantity, they can encourage a classmate to wait a few minutes until the next game because there aren't any more board game pieces available.

Creating Opportunities for Social, Emotional, and Mathematical Development Throughout the Day

To proactively help children develop social and emotional skills along with math skills throughout the day, help them understand how useful math can be in solving problems in the classroom and on the playground. For example, ask how children can take turns in teams of two, use timers to support turn taking, split popular toys into two or three equal sets, minimize frustration by counting to calm down, and rotate who goes first among children (Copley 2010; Shillady 2012). In *The Intentional Teacher,* Ann S. Epstein has a terrific section on meaningful teaching in mathematics that includes activities to support social and emotional development, like encouraging reflection and self-correction, playing games, and encouraging peer interaction. Summarizing research on how social interaction improves mathematical thinking, she writes, "When children share hypotheses and interpretations, question one another, and are challenged to justify their conclusions, they are more likely to correct their own thinking" (Epstein 2014, 131). To help teachers cultivate more math-based interactions, the following sections share ideas for small group activities, block centers, and outdoor play.

Small Group Activities

Small group activities—such as playing Chutes and Ladders, a type of game that significantly increases children's numerical knowledge (Ramani, Siegler, & Hitti 2012)—can promote an array of social and emotional skills. Successful play requires children to take turns, cooperate, and regulate their emotions.

To help children further develop skills, purposefully create engaging group activities that explore mathematics while requiring collaboration and communication. For example, draw a dinosaur to scale on the playground and then ask children to measure and compare its attributes in teams. For an indoor activity, hide a set of number cards around the classroom in a treasure hunt and then ask children to put them in order. To promote math talk among children, ask children to pair up or form small groups to work on math activities such as puzzles, tangrams, number memory games, or board games.

Block Centers

Block centers are frequently associated with promoting mathematical understanding in young children. As children investigate how many triangle-shaped blocks fit on top of a square-shaped block or the number of columnar blocks they need to support a road built with long rectangular blocks, they are counting, comparing and contrasting, measuring, estimating, and exploring geometric concepts—activities that foster mathematical development. At the same time, children's block play promotes key social and emotional skills. If you've ever carefully watched a group of children build an elaborate castle, dragon den, or race course, you know that it takes initiative, thinking about another's point of view, collaboration, and self-regulation. These constructions, which can engage children for long periods of time across several days, can be a great source of pride.

The Mathematics of Fairness

A word on fairness—an important social-awareness concept. In many ways, early childhood experiences center on fairness. Children at this age are highly tuned into circumstances that might not be fair, such as whose turn it is, who gets to go first, or how much time is allotted in sharing toys. Understanding if resources (including toys and time) have been distributed fairly frequently requires mathematical problem solving. Dividing a set of DUPLO train cars equally between two children in the block area requires counting and sharing. Knowing who gets the next turn requires some knowledge of ordinality. For activities or environments that limit the number of children who can participate (for instance, the dramatic play area) or have limited resources, counting or using a timer can ensure fairness while supporting mathematical concepts.

Mr. Luna's class has been working on turning the block area into an undersea castle. Many of the children have decorated the walls with paintings of shellfish, octopi, and seahorses in tall strands of seaweed. While some children build the castle, others populate it with miniature plastic fish and painted paper coral. Mr. Luna talks with the children about science and mathematics (how seahorses move in the water, how many fish make a school) and how the sea and castle construction wouldn't be possible without everyone working together. The children beam with pride and call out, "Take a picture of our castle! Take a picture!"

Outdoor Play

The outdoor environment abounds with opportunities for learning socially, emotionally, and mathematically. Hopscotch, for example, provides experiences with one-to-one correspondence, numeral identification, and spatial thinking while also supporting the development of self-regulation and turn taking. Physical activities like hopping and basketball not only promote number sense ("How many baskets can I make?") but also develop a deepening sense of self-confidence ("I made two more than yesterday!"). Collaborative sandbox play requires cooperation and goal setting and can support the development of measurement and geometry skills.

Conclusion

Early childhood is an important period for the development of social and emotional skills and for building a foundation rich in mathematical understanding. Educators have many opportunities to support these important domains simultaneously. Classrooms that provide engaging and mathematically rich environments, abundant and meaningful math talk, and carefully chosen math activities that support initiative, self-regulation, and collaboration will result in children gaining mathematical knowledge and developing important social and emotional skills.

REFERENCES

Copley, J.V. 2010. *The Young Child and Mathematics.* 2nd ed. Washington, DC: NAEYC.

Copley, J.V. 2014. "Goals for Early Mathematics Teachers." In *Preparing Early Childhood Educators to Teach Math: Professional Development That Works,* eds. H.P. Ginsburg, M. Hyson, & T.A. Woods, 75–96. Baltimore: Brookes.

Epstein, A.S. 2014. *The Intentional Teacher: Choosing the Best Strategies for Young Children's Learning.* Rev. ed. Washington, DC: NAEYC.

Frye, D., A.J. Baroody, M. Burchinal, S.M. Carver, N.C. Jordan, & J. McDowell. 2013. *Teaching Math to Young Children: Educator's Practice Guide.* Washington, DC: National Center for Education Evaluation and Regional Assistance, Institute of Education Sciences, US Department of Education.

IOM (Institute of Medicine) & NRC (National Research Council). 2015. *Transforming the Workforce for Children Birth Through Age 8: A Unifying Foundation.* Washington, DC: The National Academies Press.

Jackson, J. 2012. "Partnering to Bring Social and Emotional Learning to School." Commentary. *Social Policy Report* 26 (4): 27–28.

Jones, S.M., & S.M. Bouffard. 2012. "Social and Emotional Learning in Schools: From Programs to Strategies." *Social Policy Report* 26 (4): 1–22.

NAEYC. 2022. *Developmentally Appropriate Practice in Early Childhood Programs Serving Children from Birth Through Age 8.* 4th ed. Washington, DC: NAEYC.

NAEYC & NCTM (National Council of Teachers of Mathematics). 2010. "Early Childhood Mathematics: Promoting Good Beginnings." Joint position statement. Washington, DC: NAEYC. www.naeyc.org/files/naeyc/file/positions/psmath.pdf.

NRC (National Research Council). 2009. *Mathematics Learning in Early Childhood: Paths Toward Excellence and Equity.* Washington: DC: The National Academies Press.

Presser, A.L., M. Clements, H.P. Ginsburg, & B. Ertle. 2015. "Big Math for Little Kids: The Effectiveness of a Preschool and Kindergarten Mathematics Curriculum." *Early Education and Development* 26 (3): 399–426.

Ramani, G.B., R.S. Siegler, & A. Hitti. 2012. "Taking It to the Classroom: Number Board Games as a Small Group Learning Activity." *Journal of Educational Psychology* 104 (3): 661–72.

Robson, S. 2016. "Self-Regulation, Metacognition, and Child- and Adult-Initiated Activity: Does It Matter Who Initiates the Task?" *Early Child Development and Care* 186 (5): 764–84.

Sarama, J., & D.H. Clements. 2009. *Early Childhood Mathematics Education Research: Learning Trajectories for Young Children.* New York: Routledge.

Shillady, A., ed. 2012. *Spotlight on Young Children: Exploring Math.* Washington, DC: NAEYC.

Zaslow, M. 2014. "General Features of Effective Professional Development: Implications for Preparing Early Educators to Teach Mathematics." In *Preparing Early Childhood Educators to Teach Math: Professional Development that Works,* eds. H.P. Ginsburg, M. Hyson, & T.A. Woods, 97–115. Baltimore: Brookes.

About the Author

Linda M. Platas, PhD, is chair of the Child and Adolescent Development Department at San Francisco State University and a member of the Development and Research in Early Mathematics Education (DREME) Network. She has worked with children and families for 30 years and is involved in international policy and research in child development and teacher education.

Reflection Questions

1. This article describes some ways social, emotional, and mathematical development are— and can be—connected. What other examples can you provide from your own early learning setting? If possible, share your examples with a colleague or other partner. For more on this topic, see the discussion about the interconnectedness of and learning across domains on pages 30–33 in *Developmentally Appropriate Practice* (2022).

2. If you work with children younger or older than those described in this article, reflect on how you might strengthen the connections between social, emotional, and mathematical development for children in that developmental period. You might refer to the relevant age-specific practice recommendations on pages 222–251 in *Developmentally Appropriate Practice* (NAEYC 2022).

3. Asking questions about math is important, but not all questions are meaningful to a young child. How can you make math talk engaging for all children, including dual language learners or children with disabilities?

4. Plan ways that you could adapt the suggestions in this article to support the mathematical development of children who live in diverse communities and cultures while also building their sense of identity and self-worth.

5. What information in this article do you think would be most useful to share with families? What kind of examples or family engagement activities might help? For background about building family partnerships, review the examples outlined on pages 150–157 in *Developmentally Appropriate Practice* (NAEYC 2022).

6. Select one suggested activity from this article and consider how to adapt and implement it within your setting, either with an individual child or with the whole class.

Photographs: pp. 98, 100, 103, © Getty Images

Partnering with Families

Supporting Social and Emotional Development Through Picture Books

Alison Hooper

Has a family member ever asked you for tips on reducing a child's challenging behavior? Or maybe for strategies to talk to their child about something they saw on the news? Perhaps they've sought activities to help their child develop empathy and learn about diversity? While there are many ways families can support social and emotional development, picture books are one powerful teaching tool. You can encourage families to support their children's social and emotional development by reading and talking about picture books.

Many families are aware of the importance of reading to their children to support language and literacy growth, but they may not realize all of the developmental opportunities that reading together creates. For example, when a parent spends time talking with a child about the illustrations in a book—paying attention to the child's thoughts and feelings—that builds the parent-child bond.

Topics that can be challenging to talk about, like bullying or jealousy, may be easier to address with a good book as a tool. However, it can take practice to know how to start these conversations. Many families also benefit from support around how to find and pick appropriate books in different formats (print as well as digital books) and to embed meaningful conversations about these topics into their time reading together.

Here are three strategies you (as the teacher) can use to help families turn picture books into tools to prompt rich conversations about expressing feelings, gaining self-esteem, showing perseverance, and many other important skills.

Provide a Lending Library

Establish a lending library in your classroom or school with picture books that families can check out to read at home with their child. Along with each book, develop a simple discussion guide for families. Include a few open-ended questions that families can ask and a brief activity they can do together after reading. Consider keeping your lending library in a front office space, laminating and cleaning discussion guides between uses, and cleaning books and placing them in individual zip-top bags to help meet health and safety guidelines.

Here are some books you could include in your lending library, along with sample discussion guides and sample activities.

Yo! Yes? by Chris Raschka

TOPIC: FRIENDSHIP

Note for reading: This book is great if you read it with lots of expression! Your child may ask you to read it over and over. Many children understand the story better and remember more details after listening to a book a few times. And, the more times you read this book aloud, the easier it will be for you to express the characters' emotions.

Sample Discussion Questions

> How would you describe the two characters? How were they similar? How were they different?

> How did you feel about the end of the story? Why?

> What are some things that you say when you make a new friend?

Sample Extension Activity

> On the third or fourth reading, encourage your child to tell (from memory) or read one of the parts of the story while you read the other. It doesn't matter if they say or read the words perfectly!

> Write your own simple story of friendship with your child. What will the two characters say to each other?

I'm Happy-Sad Today: Making Sense of Mixed-Together Feelings, by Lory Britain, illustrated by Matthew Rivera

Sample Discussion Questions

> What were some of the feelings you heard about in the story?

> What were some of the things the girl in the story did to show her feelings? Do you like to do any of those things?

> Can you think of a time you felt two feelings together? Tell me about it.

Sample Extension Activity

With your child, pick one of the strategies for expressing feelings from the story (e.g., talking about them, pretend play, dancing, painting) and do it together. Talk about how you are feeling and why it is important to express feelings.

It's Okay to Be Different, by Todd Parr

TOPIC: SELF-CONCEPT

Sample Discussion Questions

> Do you do or like any of the same things as the characters in the story?

> What are some good things about being different?

> What are some ways that you and I are different?

Sample Extension Activity

With your child, draw pictures or create collages showing what makes each of you unique.

All Are Welcome, by Alexandra Penfold, illustrated by Suzanne Kaufman

TOPIC: SIMILARITIES AND DIFFERENCES

Sample Discussion Questions

> What do you think it means to be welcome somewhere?

> How does being welcome make you feel?

> How were the children in the story similar? What were some ways they were different?

Sample Extension Activity

> Help your child pick one place in the world to learn about and visit the library or look online together to explore similarities and differences.

> Think about what you might do to help make someone who is new to your school or community feel welcome.

One, **by Kathryn Otoshi**

Sample Discussion Questions

› How did Red act at the beginning of the story? And at the end?

› What did the number 1 do in the story when Red was mean?

› Has someone ever been mean to you or to someone else? What can you do if you see someone bullying?

Sample Extension Activity

Find different colored objects or papers around your house. Use these to act out the story with your child. Point out how the other colors stood up for themselves and how Red learned that everyone counts.

Highlight a Book in Your Communications with Families

If you have a class or program-wide newsletter, email, or social media page, select a picture book to highlight weekly or monthly. Try to select a book that families will be able to access easily, such as those you have in your school library, those available at a nearby public library, or through a library-affiliated e-book app. Share the title, a social or emotional skill to highlight, and a few questions families could use when talking to their child about the book.

You could also invite families to share their experiences doing these read alouds and include their reflections and strategies in future newsletters.

Hold a Family Literacy Event

Family literacy events are a fun way to share the many different benefits of reading together. You could include a short workshop about how to use books to start conversations with children about social and emotional topics, especially any topics that may relate to current events or to your local community. For example, families may be interested in learning about books and strategies that can help them talk to their children about race or COVID-19. If possible, give families a chance to try out the strategies you introduce while reading with their child during the event.

Family literacy events work well in person or online—you could hold an event using an online platform like Zoom, Google Hangouts, or Facebook Live. Consider recording it so that families who miss it (or who want to watch it again) can view it.

Here is a possible structure you could use for a family literacy event. (Note: This structure can be adapted for virtual workshops as well.)

> **Families attend a workshop** while their children spend time playing with program staff or volunteers. Families learn about the advantages and importance of reading aloud, strategies to use when reading aloud, and how to target social and emotional development.

> **Families receive a picture book and discussion guide,** then spend a few minutes thinking about how they will use it with their child. You can invite families to share their ideas and model a few strategies they could try.

> **Children join their families.** Families read with their children using their new book and discussion strategies. Everyone enjoys snacks and conversation, and you can walk around to answer any questions families have.

REFERENCE

NAEYC. 2022. *Developmentally Appropriate Practice in Early Childhood Programs Serving Children from Birth Through Age 8.* 4th ed. Washington, DC: NAEYC.

About the Author

Alison Hooper, PhD, is an assistant professor of early childhood education at the University of Alabama. She researches early care and education quality and professional development for early educators.

Reflection Questions

1. The article lists specific social and emotional benefits when adults share relevant picture books with children in a warm family setting. With a colleague or other partner, identify one book that might help a family discuss an emotionally important issue with a child. Role-play a book-reading interaction that might support a child's understanding of the issue while also nurturing the family-child relationship.

2. Plan a family literacy event using or adapting suggestions from this article to fit your own context. Implement your plan, if possible, and assess the results. When making decisions about the event, keep in mind the considerations about reciprocal family partnerships presented on pages 147–149 in *Developmentally Appropriate Practice* (2022).

3. With a colleague or other partner, develop a list of picture books that fits well with the interests, experiences, and characteristics of the children you teach; supports their social and emotional competence; and can be shared with children's families.

4. Does your program have a lending library, as suggested in this article? If not, what are some alternate ways you can share high-quality picture books that families can explore with their children at home? If you do have a lending library, evaluate if it includes some of the books identified above.

5. If you have families in your program whose home language is not English, how might you adapt these suggestions to affirm their culture and continue building on their children's social and emotional strengths? You might draw on the discussion of cultural differences and families' funds of knowledge on pages 55–58 in *Developmentally Appropriate Practice* (2022).

6. Some family members may have reading difficulties and hesitate to engage in book reading. Share ideas with a colleague or other partner for how you might encourage the participation of these family members in literacy events and activities (e.g., wordless picture books).

Paired Learning

Strategies for Enhancing Social Competence in Dual Language Classrooms

Iliana Alanís and María Guadalupe Arreguín

Emergent bilingual kindergartners Samuel and Efrain are engaged in an English-language math card game. Efrain chooses two cards (5 and 2) and counts the pictures on each card to determine the sum. He places his finger on each picture as he counts.

Efrain: Six. It's six.

Efrain looks at Samuel, who is shaking his head no.

Samuel: No, it's . . .

Efrain: ¡No, no. Espérate! (No, no. Wait!)

Efrain pulls the cards closer and begins to recount. Samuel patiently waits for Efrain to recount the pictures, saying each number softly along with Efrain.

Efrain: Seven.

Samuel nods yes. Efrain grins from ear to ear. Samuel takes his turn to continue the game.

Effective early childhood teachers recognize the value of developing children's social skills to promote cooperation and collaboration. They help children learn to share, take turns, and express caring for others. In this article, we (the two authors) demonstrate how teachers can guide children to develop the social competence shown in the opening vignette. We share strategies for structuring paired learning to promote cooperation and build children's social competence. We present these ideas through multiple vignettes based on our observations of numerous Spanish-English dual language practitioners in preschool through first grade classrooms. Although we concentrate on dual language settings, any teacher can implement these strategies to facilitate young children's social skill development.

With over 20 years in the early childhood field, each of us is engaged in three major roles: (1) we prepare preservice teachers within a university setting for culturally efficacious work; (2) we research teachers' daily practice within bilingual (Spanish-English) early childhood settings; and (3) we offer professional development, including coaching, on dual language instruction for teachers in preschool and elementary classrooms across the country. The majority of the teachers we work with are in programs that have Spanish-dominant and English-dominant children side by side learning content in two languages with the goals of bilingualism, biliteracy, and biculturalism.

In these roles, we observe the variety of ways teachers in dual language classrooms organize their instruction to enhance children's linguistic, academic, and social development. One crucial cooperative structure implemented in many classrooms is paired learning. Although an effective strategy, it can be challenging for children if teachers do not provide structure and guidance (Alanís 2018). Thus, our research has focused on the effective interactive strategies early childhood teachers use in dual language classrooms when pairing children for learning (Alanís 2011, 2013; Alanís & Arreguín-Anderson 2015).

When we share our research findings with educators through professional development, some frequently asked questions include

> How can I get young children to learn with a partner if they don't have the required social skills?

> How can I ask children to take turns if they are still learning to self-regulate their feelings and behaviors?

> How can I ask children to express their thoughts if they may not know how to put their thoughts into words?

Social Competence and Paired Learning

Social competence includes the social, emotional, and cognitive knowledge and skills children need to be effective in their interactions with others (Rose-Krasnor & Denham 2009). It encompasses an array of behaviors, such as interpersonal skills, self-regulation, planning, organizing, and decision making. When children willingly support and assist one another, they engage in cooperative activity—and they demonstrate and boost their social competence.

To support children's social learning, teachers should provide many opportunities for children to work and learn together. As a cooperative strategy, paired learning helps children become successful in their social interactions and is based on the following principles of sociocultural theory (Vygotsky 1978):

> Learning is social; to advance children's knowledge, interaction with teachers and peers is important.

> Social development underlies all other areas of development (linguistic, cognitive, and emotional).

> Social interactions improve social competence.

> Children develop social competence through social interaction.

Because learning is a social process, pairs provide a structure for learning in an enjoyable, relaxed setting. Children's social development is supported by more competent others (including peers and teachers) through interactions within a social context. Paired learning lends itself to social interaction in which partners provide assistance, guidance, and direction through scaffolding and social construction of knowledge (Burman 2009; Mooney 2000).

How Can Teachers Help Children Develop Social Skills?

In previous work, we discussed how teachers intentionally partner children based on their strengths (Alanís 2018; Alanís & Arreguin-Anderson 2015). These strengths include their language capabilities, their conceptual understandings, and their personalities. Pairing children heterogeneously allows students to learn by observing or participating with a peer—the more knowledgeable other (Vygotsky 1978). Partners can provide support if children are matched with a peer who is just a little bit above their current level of understanding, or zone of proximal development.

Within these heterogeneous partnerships, children are responsible for each other's learning. This presumes that each child has the capability to teach and learn and that each child has something important to contribute. It also sends a strong message of high expectations for young learners. How the teacher structures the task, however, can support or hinder children's success (Alanís 2018).

Young children come to school with varying levels of cooperative skills. Some children are already capable of compromising, taking turns, and listening to a partner, while others are still developing these skills. Some children may be reluctant to talk because their expressive language is still developing. Thus, in the following sections we highlight the significance of providing explicit modeling, focusing on one skill at a time, and creating multiple opportunities for children to practice these new skills. We also remind teachers of the need to provide a variety of visual scaffolds for young children to "see" what is expected of them.

Provide Explicit Modeling

Teacher modeling shows children what they are to do and helps children work together more effectively (Alanís 2018). Teachers can model the behavior they want to establish by demonstrating a specific activity and related expectations. While visiting Mrs. Kelly's bilingual kindergarten class, we observed as she assembled the children on the carpet and asked them to watch while she presented a new center activity: matching picture cards to words. She slowly took cards out of a baggie and placed them in front of her. She showed children how to complete the activity as she talked them through it:

> "When you shuffle the cards, don't do it very fast. Take it easy and go slowly," Mrs. Kelly explains. Then, she asks Marco and Sandra to come show her and the rest of the class how they are supposed to play with the materials. Mrs. Kelly begins by asking, "Who is going to take out the materials?" Marco points to Sandra. "Good, Marco, you are letting your partner do it; but remember to take turns taking the materials out and putting them away."

> Next, Mrs. Kelly asks Marco to shuffle the cards. She invites Sandra to help him. As Sandra is shuffling, Marco says, "Take it easy, go slowly," using the language and behavior Mrs. Kelly modeled.

As the rest of the children watched, Mrs. Kelly walked Marco and Sandra through the process of taking turns while playing the game. She focused on turn taking and language use:

> Mrs. Kelly tells the two, "When you pick up a card, read it and ask your partner to find the matching picture. Try it, Marco. Pick a card and read the word on the card." Marco picks a card and reads, "Elefante" (Elephant). Mrs. Kelly says, "Good. Now ask Sandra to find the matching picture." Marco asks Sandra, "¿Dónde está?" (Where is it?), as he shows her the picture card.

> Sandra searches through the cards until she finds the picture of an elephant. "What is it, Sandra?" Mrs. Kelly asks. Sandra replies, "An elephant." "That's right!" says Mrs. Kelly. "Place it next to Marco's card." Mrs. Kelly reminds the children to make sure their partner is correct, adding, "You can help, but let them try first."

After Marco and Sandra modeled the game a couple of times for the whole class, Mrs. Kelly asked each pair of students to go to their tables while she distributed the game materials.

Taking the time to have a pair of students model for the class was a crucial step; it showed the children the expectations for language use and behavior during partner learning. It also allowed Mrs. Kelly to determine whether children understood the required behavior before she had them do the activity on their own (reducing the need for teacher mediation).

Some details to explain through modeling include the following:

> Who goes first?

> How do we share the materials?

> Do we share a pencil? Paper?

> What do we say to each other?

> When should we take turns?

> Where do we place the materials once we finish with the activity?

Focus on One Skill at a Time

Teachers can help children identify exactly what they need to do by planning a structured activity to practice a specific skill. We observed an excellent example in Mr. Sanchez's bilingual first-grade classroom during an English language activity. Mr. Sanchez sat his students on the carpet in front of him and asked if they liked having someone read to them. The children responded with a resounding "Yes!" Then Mr. Sanchez introduced partner reading:

> Mr. Sanchez explains, "Today you and your partner will read a book together by taking turns. Let me show you." He asks Veronica to join him. "I'm going to read one page, and Veronica is going to read the next one." He begins to read, using his finger to track the words. Then Mr. Sanchez says, "Okay, Veronica—now it's your turn." Veronica slowly reads the next page, with some help from Mr. Sanchez. Mr. Sanchez then continues to the next page. "That's how we help each other and take turns," he says. "Now, how are you going to take turns reading?"
>
> Several students respond in unison, "I read one page and my partner reads one page." Mr. Sanchez confirms their answer: "That's correct. You have to take turns reading to each other. That way, both of you are learning new words as you take turns. Okay, I'll give each pair a book and you and your partner can find a quiet place in the room to sit and read together."

Taking turns and sharing are examples of behaviors children use regularly, if encouraged to do so. By pairing children to read a book together, teachers create opportunities for children to practice early reading behaviors in an informal manner that benefits both partners. These activities build specific social skills—in this case, turn taking—as they provide integrated learning opportunities for language and literacy.

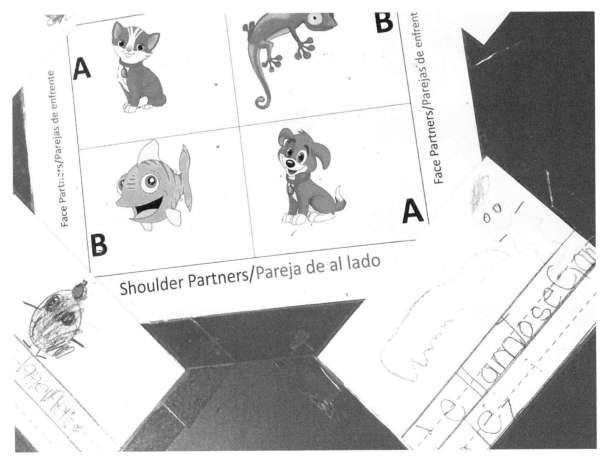

Create Opportunities for Collaborative Interaction

Play is the dominant form of social activity in early childhood classrooms. Play and social learning have a complex relationship, with new learning occurring in the context of play and then practiced during subsequent play (Kostelnik et al. 2018). During play, children engage in complex social interactions as they develop roles to enact in their play and decide the details of what to play.

Sociodramatic play is one of the most common forms of play found in early childhood classrooms. As children negotiate and take on different roles related to the theme, pretend play facilitates interpersonal skills and improves children's creativity and cognitive development (Axelrod 2014). Because children learn more easily in situations that are familiar to them, teachers can create centers with props from familiar settings, such as a bakery, a restaurant, or a local supermarket (Salinas-Gonzalez, Arreguín-Anderson, & Alanís 2017).

In Ms. Vogelpohl's bilingual pre-K classroom, the dramatic play center has become a bakery. Ms. Vogelpohl has created scenes of winter and has infused scents of cinnamon to enhance children's experiences in the dramatic play center. When children arrive at the center, they quickly organize their kitchen utensils and toppings for their gingerbread men. Karla, Mario, Diego, and Patricia engage in role-play. Mario takes on the role of baker, Patricia as the assistant, and Karla and Diego as customers.

Mario: Saca las bandejas para comenzar. (Take out the pans to start.)

Patricia reaches for a muffin tin and a cookie sheet and places them on the table, while Mario fixes his apron.

Karla: Yo quiero chocolate y marshmallows. (I want chocolate and marshmallows.)

Diego: ¡Yo también! (Me too!)

Patricia gathers the toppings and offers them to Karla.

The process of directing, requesting, and coordinating efforts led to organized play and created a shared goal of making gingerbread cookies. Although Patricia (a native Spanish speaker) said very little during the play scenario, she participated with and understood her English-speaking classmates. Within the bakery center, Ms. Vogelpohl encouraged and facilitated social interactions so that all of the children engaged in roles that were comfortable for their level of linguistic and social development (Alanís & Arreguín-Anderson 2015).

While dramatic play is an important means of creating opportunities for children to interact, teachers sometimes have specific topics that they would like children to discuss in order to build language, vocabulary, and social skills. To achieve these goals, teachers may create more structured, playful activities. Although there is no prescribed time or age at which to introduce structured interactions, teachers can closely observe children's levels of comfort and mastery of skills (such as turn taking and maintaining eye contact) to gradually involve them in more complex interactions. For example, across the hall from Ms. Vogelpohl, Mrs. Lara used musical partners to combine music, movement, and discussion.

The strategy of musical partners begins with children dancing while music plays. When the music stops children high-five the person closest to them and discuss a question or topic the teacher has provided. When the music starts up again, the children thank each other and dance around until the music stops.

The process starts over, with children each high-fiving a new partner. This gets the children used to engaging with different partners in an enjoyable and stress-free environment. Reminding children to say *thank you* also encourages mutual respect.

The musical partners strategy creates opportunities for movement and for children to talk with each other about topics that connect to their interests and experiences, all while addressing specific academic objectives. Topics that easily add relevance to any lesson include children's families or pets, favorite colors or holidays, and places children have visited. As with all structured activities, gradual exposure to collaborative tasks ensures successful participation in these types of interactive endeavors.

Create Visual Scaffolds

Visual scaffolds provide critical support as children acquire new skills. A visual representation of a concept serves as a tool to access ideas that may be abstract or complex, thus facilitating comprehension. Visual scaffolds include words, drawings, pictures, diagrams, and objects. A successful strategy using visual scaffolds that we observed was the creation of an anchor chart that provided cues for what working with a partner should look and sound like. An *anchor chart* is a teaching element developed with students that provides gentle reminders of expectations and routines. Teachers create these visuals as a class activity, with children contributing their own ideas. Effective anchor charts are visually appealing, clearly focused, and effectively use text and images to illustrate the key concept.

When we visited Mrs. Aguilera's kindergarten class, she engaged in a discussion with the children to create an anchor chart for being a good partner:

Mrs. Aguilera sits on the carpet with her class of 5-year-olds, who are dual language learners. She asks the children to tell her what they think working with a partner should look like. Children speak in the language they are most comfortable using as they give responses such as, "You should stay with your partner" and "Tienen que trabajar juntos" (You have to work together). As the children speak, Mrs. Aguilera writes their responses on chart paper—her anchor chart.

She also suggests that the children should look at their partners when they are talking to them and share materials. She then asks the children to think about what working with a partner should sound like.

The children's initial response is, "Talking, you should be talking." Mrs. Aguilera extends that idea: "Yes, you should be talking. But you should also be listening to what your partner is saying, right?" Children nod their heads in agreement.

To emphasize the listening component of the interactions, Mrs. Aguilera prompts them to think about an activity completed earlier in the day: "During math, I heard Charlie using his manners when he asked Izel for some more tiles. He said thank you when Izel gave him some tiles—remember, Charlie? So, what should it sound like when we are working with our partners?" Several children respond, "We should use our manners!"

Mrs. Aguilera continues prompting students. Eventually, the class agrees that working with a partner should sound like "saying nice things to your partner," "saying please and thank you," "saying excuse me," and "listening."

The creation of the anchor chart enabled Mrs. Aguilera to hear children's ideas as they constructed their own understandings of paired learning. Mrs. Aguilera placed the chart in an accessible location so that students could use it as a visual reminder when needed.

Another effective strategy we have observed is the use of sentence frames. It is often difficult for young children to organize their ideas into words, especially if they are doing so in their second language. Providing developmentally appropriate and linguistically accessible sentence frames helps children engage in structured conversations.

Mrs. Vasquez's group of emergent bilingual 4-year-olds is seated on the carpet as she reads a story about selling apples at the market. Mrs. Vasquez pauses to talk about the different types of apples in the story and indicates that her favorites are sour green apples. She then asks the children to turn to their partners and ask them, "¿Qué tipos de manzanas te gustan?" (What types of apples do you like?) Children turn their bodies so they are facing their partners and initiate the exchange: "¿Qué tipos de manzanas te gustan?" Children can be heard saying, "A mí me gustan las verdes" (I like the green ones), "Rojas" (The red ones), and "¡Todas!" (All of them!).

In this situation, the sentence frame helped children with the skill of asking and responding to a question. Although several children responded with one-word answers, the turn-and-talk strategy gave them an opportunity to hear their partners ask the question and to listen to their classmates respond to it. The next time Mrs. Vasquez asks her students to turn and talk, she could also provide a sentence frame for the reply, such as, "A mí me gustan las manzanas _____" (I like the _____ apples). This enables children to practice the authentic use of new words and skills as they learn the reciprocal action of a conversation.

Teachers can post sentence frames on chart paper or on students' desks so that children can refer to them when they need to. The following are some initial stems to get students started:

> What do you think will happen next? I think _____.

> Which story did you like? I liked _____.

> Who was your favorite character? My favorite character was _____.

> In my opinion, _____. I agree with you/I disagree with you because_____.

Conclusion

Young children's social development requires intentional modeling from a teacher, opportunities to practice new skills, and scaffolding. When teachers structure paired learning effectively, it has the potential to develop language, content knowledge, and social skills (Arreguín-Anderson & Alanís 2017). A primary benefit for young children, however, is the power to develop competency in their social skills—a precursor to all other forms of learning (Riley & Jones 2010).

The teaching practices in these vignettes reflect language-rich classrooms where all children are encouraged to develop their social competence in comfortable and engaging settings. These social structures are important and valuable because all learners need opportunities to interact with each other as part of their learning experiences.

REFERENCES

Alanís, I. 2018. "Enhancing Collaborative Learning: Activities and Structures in a Dual Language Preschool Classroom." *Association of Mexican American Educators (AMAE) Journal* 12 (1): 5–26.

Alanís, I. 2011. "Learning from Each Other: Bilingual Pairs in Dual-Language Classrooms." *Dimensions of Early Childhood* 39 (1): 21–28.

Alanís, I. 2013. "Where's Your Partner? Pairing Bilingual Learners in Preschool and Primary Grade Dual Language Classrooms." *Young Children* 68 (1): 42–46.

Alanís, I., & M.G. Arreguín-Anderson. 2015. "Developing Paired Learning in Dual Language Classrooms." *Early Years* 36 (1): 24–28.

Arreguín-Anderson, M.G., & I. Alanís. 2017. "Oral Academic Language by Design: Bilingual Pre-service Teachers' Purposeful Infusion of Paired Strategies During Science Instruction." *Journal of Classroom Interaction* 52 (2): 31–44.

Axelrod, Y. 2014. "'Todos Vamos a Jugar, Even the Teachers'—Everyone Playing Together." *Young Children* 69 (2): 24–31.

Burman, L. 2009. *Are You Listening? Fostering Conversations That Help Young Children Learn*. St. Paul, MN: Redleaf.

Kostelnik, M.J., A.K. Soderman, A.P. Whiren, & M.L. Rupiper. 2018. *Guiding Children's Social Development and Learning: Theory and Skills*. 9th ed. Stamford, CT: Cengage Learning.

Mooney, C.G. 2000. *Theories of Childhood: An Introduction to Dewey, Montessori, Erikson, Piaget, and Vygotsky*. St. Paul, MN: Redleaf.

NAEYC. 2022. *Developmentally Appropriate Practice in Early Childhood Programs Serving Children from Birth Through Age 8*. 4th ed. Washington, DC: NAEYC.

Riley, J.G., & R.B. Jones. 2010. "Acknowledging Learning Through Play in the Primary Grades." *Childhood Education* 86 (3): 146–49.

Rose-Krasnor, L., & S. Denham. 2009. "Social–Emotional Competence in Early Childhood." In *Handbook of Peer Interactions, Relationships, and Groups*, eds. K.H. Rubin, W.M. Bukowski, & B. Laursen, 162–79. New York: Guilford.

Salinas-Gonzalez, I., M.G. Arreguín-Anderson, & I. Alanís. 2017. "Supporting Language: Culturally Rich Dramatic Play." *Teaching Young Children* 11 (2): 4–6.

Vygotsky, L.S. 1978. *Mind in Society: The Development of Higher Psychological Processes*. Cambridge, MA: Harvard University Press.

About the Authors

Iliana Alanís, PhD, is professor of early childhood and elementary education at the University of Texas at San Antonio. She conducts research in dual language early childhood settings and provides professional development for dual language educators.

María Guadalupe Arreguín, EdD, is professor of early childhood and elementary education at the University of Texas at San Antonio. Her research focuses on dual language education and interactive learning in dyads.

Reflection Questions

1. The authors describe bilingual settings with Spanish-dominant and English-dominant children learning side by side. Think about your own early learning setting. What are the similarities and differences? How might you adapt examples from this article to your setting?

2. Think about a child you teach who speaks a home language that is different than that of most of the children in the group. How does the language difference influence how other children engage with this child? How does the language difference influence this child's social relationships and their development of social competence?

3. Still thinking about the child from the previous question, how might you use some of the suggestions in this article to connect that child with others in the group so that the children begin to learn and interact together? Refer to the discussion of how to nurture children's relationships on pages 115–116 in *Developmentally Appropriate Practice* (NAEYC 2022).

4. Collaboration is identified as one of the essential skills that is nurtured through playful pedagogy. (See page 85 in *Developmentally Appropriate Practice* [NAEYC 2022].) Try out several new paired learning activities with the children you teach. Whether or not your class includes children who are dual language learners, the pairs may have many other differences or challenges in working together. Observe the pairs as they interact during an activity. What supports can you provide to help the children learn with and from one another?

5. The article authors emphasize the importance of teachers helping children to work together by explicitly demonstrating or modeling. Developmentally appropriate practice also highlights modeling among a wide range of strategies that effective teachers use; see pages 183–184 in *Developmentally Appropriate Practice* (NAEYC 2022). Consider the examples explored in the article and try out your own ways of modeling how to do a classroom activity together.

Photographs: pp. 112, 116, 118, 119, courtesy of the authors

Index

Page numbers followed by *f, t,* and *b* indicate figures, tables, and text boxes, respectively.